# PRACTICAL GUIDE TO DISCIPLINARY ACTION IN BANKS

**G.S. DUBEY**
*Advocate,*
*Former Manager (Law),*
*Central Bank of India.*
***E-mail:*** *gslawhel@gmail.com*

**FIRST EDITION : 2014**

Himalaya Publishing House

MUMBAI • NEW DELHI • NAGPUR • BENGALURU • HYDERABAD • CHENNAI • PUNE • LUCKNOW • AHMEDABAD • ERNAKULAM • BHUBANESWAR • INDORE • KOLKATA • GUWAHATI

**First Edition : 2014**

**Edition : 2017**

---

**Published by** : Mrs. Meena Pandey for **Himalaya Publishing House Pvt. Ltd.**, "Ramdoot", Dr. Bhalerao Marg, Girgaon, **Mumbai - 400 004.**
Phone: 022-23860170/23863863, Fax: 022-23877178
**E-mail: himpub@vsnl.com; Website: www.himpub.com**

**Branch Offices** :

**New Delhi** : "Pooja Apartments", 4-B, Murari Lal Street, Ansari Road, Darya Ganj, New Delhi - 110 002.
Phone: 011-23270392, 23278631; Fax: 011-23256286

**Nagpur** : Kundanlal Chandak Industrial Estate, Ghat Road, Nagpur - 440 018.
Phone: 0712-2738731, 3296733; Telefax: 0712-2721216

**Bengaluru** : No. 16/1 (Old 12/1), 1st Floor, Next to Hotel Highlands, Madhava Nagar, Race Course Road, Bengaluru - 560 001.
Phone: 080-22286611, 22385461, 4113 8821, 22281541

**Hyderabad** : No. 3-4-184, Lingampally, Besides Raghavendra Swamy Matham, Kachiguda, Hyderabad - 500 027. Phone: 040-27560041, 27550139

**Chennai** : 8/2 Madley 2nd street, T. Nagar, Chennai - 600 017. Mobile: 09320490962

**Pune** : First Floor, "Laksha" Apartment, No. 527, Mehunpura, Shaniwarpeth (Near Prabhat Theatre), Pune - 411 030.
Phone: 020-24496323/24496333; Mobile: 09370579333

**Lucknow** : House No 731, Shekhupura Colony, Near B.D. Convent School, Aliganj, Lucknow - 226 022. Phone: 0522-4012353; Mobile: 09307501549

**Ahmedabad** : 114, "SHAIL", 1st Floor, Opp. Madhu Sudan House, C.G. Road, Navrang Pura, Ahmedabad - 380 009.
Phone: 079-26560126; Mobile: 09377088847

**Ernakulam** : 39/176 (New No: 60/251) 1st Floor, Karikkamuri Road, Ernakulam, Kochi – 682011. Phone: 0484-2378012, 2378016; Mobile: 09387122121

**Bhubaneswar** : 5 Station Square, Bhubaneswar - 751 001 (Odisha).
Phone: 0674-2532129, Mobile: 09338746007

**Indore** : Kesardeep Avenue Extension, 73, Narayan Bagh, Flat No. 302, IIIrd Floor, Near Humpty Dumpty School, Indore - 452 007 (M.P.). Mobile: 09303399304

**Kolkata** : 108/4, Beliaghata Main Road, Near ID Hospital, Opp. SBI Bank, Kolkata - 700 010, Phone: 033-32449649, Mobile: 7439040301

**Guwahati** : House No. 15, Behind Pragjyotish College, Near Sharma Printing Press, P.O. Bharalumukh, Guwahati - 781009, (Assam).
Mobile: 09883055590, 08486355289, 7439040301

**DTP by** : **Apte & Asha**

**Printed at** : Geetanjali Press Pvt. Ltd., Kundanlal Chandak Industrial Estate, Ghat Road, Nagpur - 440 018.

*This work is dedication to*
*my respected father*
*Lt. Pandit Prem Chand Dubey*

# PREFACE

Disciplinary Action/Proceedings has been subject of many law books and some of them are enough bulky. The present work has been prepared keeping in view the requirements of personnel departments in public sector banks as well as the defending officer employee. The object of the book is that Disciplinary Action/Proceedings may be carried out in a smooth manner and the same can be achieved only when parties to action understand their position in the proceedings. Further, an introduction to many concepts like probation, vigilance etc. has been given to augment the usefulness of the book for officer of the Bank.

I acknowledge the contribution received from friends particularly Mr. M.C. Vyas, Retd. Chief Manager, Central Bank of India.

I hope the work will be useful in day-to-day working for all concerned.

I am awaiting your response and precious advice for betterment of the work in coming editions.

***G.S. Dubey***

*T-4 Jhoomar Ghat Colony*
*Near Hotel Mashal*
*Rau, Indore (M.P.)*
*Ph. 0731-4245808, 09893601679*
***E-mail:*** *gslawhel@gmail.com*

# CONTENTS

## PART I

**PART II**

# PART I

# CHAPTER 1

# PUBLIC SECTOR BANKS AND THEIR CONDUCT RULES

## 1. About Officer of Bank and his Misconduct

Indian Banking industry consist of various kinds of banks including foreign banks. Reserve Bank of India is regulatory and statutory authority and controller in Banking industry. Table given below depicts the structure of Indian banking Sector:

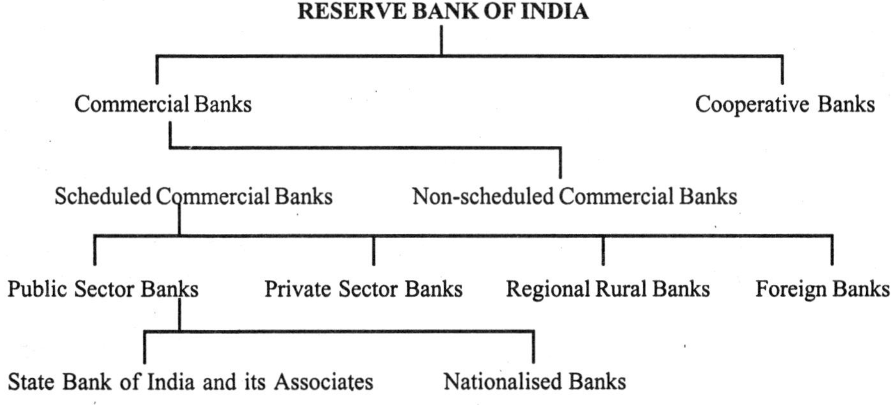


Although the disciplinary action/procedure runs on the almost same route banking sector and as well as other financial institutes but considering the number of employees in public sector banks, reference is made to them.

The concept of public sector banks means and includes —

I. A Nationalised Bank

II. State Bank of India

III. Subsidiaries of State Bank of India

IV. Any other Bank which may be declared by Government

The management of all public sector banks has been vested in their Board of Directors. Board of Directors has general powers of superintendence, directions and management of affairs of the concerned Banking Institution. Further, Government has granted managerial autonomy and therefore Government has no day-to-day control over personnel matters in public sector banks. So far as nationalised banks are concerned, the same have been established under the Banks Nationalisation Act (Act No. 5 of 1970) wherein the nationalised banks have been described as 'corresponding new bank'. It has been provided that on the commencement of the said Act, they shall be constituted such corresponding new banks as are specified in the First Schedule. In sub-section (2) of Section 3, it is laid down that the paid-up capital of every corresponding new bank constituted under sub-section (1) shall, until any provision is made in this behalf in any scheme made under Section 9, be equal to the paid-up capital of the existing bank in relation to which it is the corresponding new bank. Sub-section 3 of Section 3 provides that the entire capital of the new bank shall stand vested in, and allotted to the Central Government. Sub-section (4) of Section 6 lays down that every corresponding new bank shall be a body corporate with perpetual succession and a common seal with power, subject to the provisions of the said Act, to acquire, hold and dispose of property, and to contract, and may sue and be sued in its name. From the aforesaid provisions contained in Section 3 of the Banks Nationalisation Act, it is evident that the nationalised banks have been established under the provisions of the said Act and the same are distinct juristic persons with perpetual succession and the power to acquire, hold and dispose of property and to contract and having the right to sue and be sued in their own name and further that the entire capital of the said banks is vested in the Central Government, meaning thereby, that the said banks are owned by the Central Government.

Whether nationalised bank is a body corporate or a corporation can be answered by referring the provisions of the Banks Nationalisation Act which show that the nationalised bank has been constituted as a distinct juristic person by the Act and it is owned by the Central Government. There are other provisions in the Banks Nationalisation Act which show that the general superintendence, direction and management of the affairs of business of the bank is vested in a Board of Directors constituted by the Central Government and the Central Government has the power to remove a person from the membership of the Board of Directors [Section 7(2) and 7(3)] and in the discharge of its functions the Bank is to be guided by such directions in regard to matters of policy involving public interest as the Central

Government may, after consultation with the Governor of the Reserve Bank of India give (Section 8). This indicates that the nationalised banks have all the attributes of the new pattern of public corporation.

Merely because the expression 'body corporate' has been used in relation to the nationalised banks in Section 3(4) of the Banks Nationalisation Act and the expression 'corporation' has not been used, does not mean that the nationalised bank is not a corporation. The expression 'body corporate' is used in legal parlance to mean 'a public or private corporation.' The conditions of service of the employees are governed by the Act and Service Regulations framed thereunder. Under Section 8 of the Act, the Bank is guided by such directions in regard to matters of policy involving public interest as the Central Government may after consultation with Governor of Reserve Bank of India given under Section 19 of the Act enables the Board of Directors to make regulations to provide for all matters for which provision is expedient even relating to duties and conduct of officers and other employees of the corresponding new Bank.

In nationalised banks, Conduct Rules are framed under Section 19 of Banking (Acquisition and Transfer of Undertakings) Act 1970 (Act No. 5 of 1970) in consultation with Reserve Bank of India and with the previous sanction of Government of India, Board of Directors must have regard to the guidelines issued by Central Government. Once a regulation is formed, it becomes part of statute book. Any breach in term of Regulation is deemed to constitute misconduct. Regulations deal with different terms of employment of service. **The officer conduct regulations** of a nationalised bank do not apply on following category of staff:

1. The Chairman of a Bank.
2. The Managing Director of a Bank.
3. Any Whole-time Director of a Bank if there is any.
4. Award staff including casual labourers paid from contingencies.

Once Banks have framed Regulations pertaining to the terms and conditions of the services of the Officers, any circular of Government having not been adopted by Board of Director, in contradiction of Regulation of the Bank, will not be effective. Any such direction of Government will be liable to be ignored.[1] De hors, the Regulations, there is no power vested in the Bank to issue directions relating to conditions of service of its employee.[2]

In terms of Regulations, drawing up a charge sheet by the Disciplinary Authority is the first step for initiation of disciplinary action. Therefore, unless and until, a charge-sheet is drawn up, Disciplinary Action/Proceedings for the purpose of Conduct Regulations cannot be initiated. Drawing up a charge-sheet is a condition precedent for initiation of Disciplinary Action/Proceedings. In absence of any

1. Apoourva Ranjan Sarkar Vs Bank of India 1995(2) Bank CLR 181 (Patna)
2. Bank of India and Others Vs Bank of India Officers' Association (A.P. Unit) and Others 1995(2) Bank CLR 189 (A.P.)

statutory rule operating in the field resorting to a preliminary inquiry would not by itself be enough to hold that a disciplinary proceeding has been initiated. Under the Conduct Regulation of Bank, a breach of any of the provisions of the Regulations is deemed to constitute misconduct punishable.

## 1. ABOUT OFFICER OF BANK AND HIS MISCONDUCT

*Who is an Officer?* – Officer is also an employee of Bank. A person who is holding a supervisory, administrative or managerial post in Bank is called an Officer. A person may become Officer either with the initial appointment or by promotion. Officer employee is a cadre, though while working in Bank, he may be designated with any other name. Even if an Officer is deputed to any other organisation, he will remain Officer and will not loose his cadre as per the posting in new institution. What is made relevant and what is required to be considered in deciding whether a person is employed in a managerial or administrative capacity is not his designation in the employment but what exactly are the duties assigned to him. Thus, an officer doing some manual or clerical work as ancillary or incidental to his employment will not become a clerk.

Similarly, though an officer may be subject to control and supervision and answerable yet it will not make his functions less managerial. A Bank officer is required to exercise higher standard of honesty and integrity. He deals with money of depositors and the customers. Every officer is required to take all possible steps to protect the interest of Bank and to discharge his duty with utmost honesty, integrity and devotion.

Good conduct and discipline are inseparable from the functioning of every officer of the Bank. The very discipline of an organisation more particularly of a Bank is dependent upon each of its officers and officers acting and operating within their allotted sphere. Acting beyond one's authority is by itself a breach of discipline and misconduct.[1]

The dictionary meaning of word '**misconduct**' is improper behaviour, intentional wrongdoing or deliberate violation of a rule of standard behaviour. The word 'misconduct' does not mean inefficiency or slackness. It is something more deliberate and intentional having involvement. Therefore, charge of misconduct is the charge of some positive act or of conduct which would be quite incompatible with the express and implied terms of relationship of the employee to the employer. Misconduct is something more than mere breach of term of the agreement or the rule. It must ordinarily be something which must impinge upon the conduct expected of an officer. Misconduct for which Disciplinary Action/Proceedings can be taken need not always be a discharge of duty in the course of employment. Conduct outside the employment may have a bearing on the employment and may constitute sufficient reason for inflicting the one of the penalties given in Conduct Regulations of Bank. Any act

1. Chairman and Managing Director, United Commercial Bank and Others Vs P.C. Kakkar 2003(1) Bank CLR 622 (S.C.)

wherever and whenever committed if it has subverting discipline or good conduct will amount to misconduct. Long back, Bombay High Court[1] highlighted the illustrated cases of acts of misconduct which will justify the dismissal of the Delinquent Officer employee:

"(i) if act or conduct is prejudicial or likely to be prejudicial to the interest of the master or to the reputation of the master;

(ii) if the act or conduct is inconsistent or incompatible with the due or peaceful discharge of his duty to his master;

(iii) if the act or conduct of a servant makes it unsafe for the employer to retain him in service;

(iv) if the act or conduct of the servant is so grossly immoral that all reasonable men will say that the employee cannot be trusted;

(v) if the act or conduct of the employee is such that the master cannot rely on the faithfulness of his employee;

(vi) if the act or conduct of the employee is such as to open before him temptations for not discharging his duties properly;

(vii) if the servant is abusive or if he disturbs the peace at the place of his employment;

(viii) if he is insulting and insubordinate to such a degree as to be incompatible with the continuance of the relation of master and servant;

(ix) if the servant is habitually negligent in respect of the duties for which he is engaged;

(x) if the neglect of the servant, though isolated, tends to cause serious consequence."

In case the allegations made against a Delinquent Officer does not constitute misconduct, the same cannot be proceeded departmentally and no penalty can be imposed. Erroneous act of an employee or error of judgment on his part will not amount to misconduct.

Misconduct generally consists of two kinds as per Conduct Regulations (Please see the Regulations of the Bank) —

I. General Misconduct

II. Special Misconduct

Now, we talk of breach of ideal conduct which will constitute general misconduct. Some of such ideal conduct examples may be —

— Officer will discharge his duties with utmost integrity, honesty, devotion and diligence.

---

1. Sharda Prasad Omkar Prasad Tiwari Vs Central Railway 1960(1) LLJ 167, (Mumbai)

— Officer will do nothing which is unbecoming of a Bank Officer.

— Officer will maintain good conduct and discipline.

— Power conferred/delegated will be utilised in the interest of Institution.

— Officer shall take steps to ensure the integrity and devotion to duty of subordinates also.

— Officer shall maintain secrecy about Bank or its customers' affairs and will not disclose any information to outsider.

— Officer will not utilise his position to procure benefit for his/her relatives/ nears.

— Officer will not do any trade or business directly or indirectly.

Code of Conduct as set out in Conduct Regulation clearly indicates the conduct expected of an officer of the Bank. It will follow that conduct which is blameworthy for the officer in the context of Conduct Rules would be misconduct. A disregard of an essential condition of the contract of service will constitute misconduct. Breach of manual of instructions, regulatory circulars, specific instructions, orders and directions will constitute misconduct. Some irregularities, recognised as misconduct in banking industry, are given below though they are not exhaustive but provide a glance as to the true nature and concept of misconduct.

**Government-sponsored Schemes**

— Issuance of fixed deposits from the cash disbursed to borrowers and recovery effected from the proceeds of the said fixed deposits on maturity.

— Loan pass books not issued to the beneficiaries.

— Receipt/borrower's certificate evidencing purchase of asset in respect of loans disbursed in case not found/not preserved or bills of purchase not obtained.

— Letters sponsoring the applications of beneficiaries under various schemes were not kept on record or not available.

— Scale of finance not adhered to.

— Financing bullock/bullock cart to ineligible borrowers.

— Financing pump sets/tractors without observing the requirement of possessing the minimum landholding by the borrower.

**Staff Loans**

— Sanctioning of housing/conveyance/personal consumer loan to staff while the earlier loan was outstanding.

— Availing overdraft against the securities pledged for Demand loan.

— Fraudulently availing Demand Loan against the deposits of others.

— Non-payment of loan installment.

**Housekeeping/Correspondence etc.**

— Not attending to controlling office correspondence.

— Lack of diligence and vigilance while taking over temporary charge of the branch.

— Non-adherence to the laid down systems and procedures leading to loss of security forms/revenue leakage etc.

— Payment of fraudulently drawn cheques/withdrawals without verifying the specimen signature recorded at the branch.

— Delayed reporting and settlement of currency transfer transactions with Reserve Bank of India.

— Passing withdrawal forms for payment without pass book.

— Failure to put through large accumulated non-responded inquiry memos.

— Delayed remittances of collections to Government departments causing loss to the Institution.

## Audit

Non-reporting of deficiencies/irregularities/balancing position in audit report.

## Advances

— Granting of credit facility beyond discretionary powers.

— Allowing drawing in cash credit (bills) account before compiling opinion report on the buyers.

— No effective pre-sanction and post-sanction visit of the units.

— Encouraging middleman in selection of borrowers.

— Inadequate follow-up of advance.

— Sanctioning of *ad hoc* limit while the account was irregular.

— Sanction of demand loans against matured and paid fixed deposits and other like securities.

— Non-verification of the security offered for pledge before sanctioned.

— End-use of funds not ensured.

— Borrowers failed to abide by stipulated repayment terms or mechanism while branch failed to enforce the same.

— Granting of credit facilities to dependants and relatives.

— Enhancement of limits in irregular loan accounts.

— Obtaining of defective securities or securities with defective title or inadequate security.

— Issuing of Bank guarantees without taking commission.

## Books and Register

— Non-maintaining of receiving Dak register particularly of the beneficiary's application for loan under Government-sponsored scheme.

— Non-recording of sanction in sanction register.

— Non-maintenance of inspection and village index register.

— Non-recording of movements in log-book/movement register.

— Non-recording of loan applications in loan application and disposal register.

— Unauthorised alterations of the names of the beneficiaries in the loan applications and control card cum ledger sheets.

— Permitting outsiders to make entries in ledgers.

— Failure to maintain token register resulting in perpetration of fraud.

— Duplicate saving bank pass book issued but not recorded on the ledger sheet.

## Staff Matters

— Non-relieving of staff who has been transferred by management.

— Opening of office and doing business at holiday.

— Non-relieving of staff for few days for assistance in another branch.

— Acting in breach of Bank circulars.

— Inclusion of increment non-available in the register.

## Negligence in Working

Charge can be sustained even if negligence by bank manager is proved which is likely to cause serious loss to Bank thus even simple negligence that nature will be gross misconduct.[1]

Likelihood of serious loss coupled with negligence is sufficient to bring the case within gross misconduct. Gross negligence or negligence likely to involve the Bank in 'serious loss' would come under major misconduct. Even assuming that there is no gross negligence, simple negligence will come under major misconduct if accompanied by 'likelihood' of serious loss.[2] There is little or no scope for an officer of Bank to take shelter under the pretext that the proved misconduct has occasioned on account of an error of judgment.

The scope of Disciplinary Action/Proceedings is confined to finding out whether or not the Delinquent Officer is a guilty of the misconduct alleged against him. The line dividing a claim made on error of judgment is too thin.

Where the Delinquent Officer tries to defraud Bank for his personal gain, it is immaterial whether the Bank has suffered any financial loss or not. It is the conduct

1. R.S. Gupta Vs State Bank of India and Others 2000(2) Bank CLR 248 (Del)
2. State Bank of India and Others Vs T.J. Paul 2000(2) Bank CLR 343, 1994(4) S.C.C. 759

which matters most and therefore Delinquent Officer cannot be treated with benevolence by giving him an opportunity to mend himself.[1]

The fact that *no loss* has been caused to the Bank that is a matter which may effect the punishment to be inflicted but not the sustainability of the specific charges framed against an employee. Where loans were granted wrongly and loan accounts are running irregularly for long, it cannot be said that no loss has been caused to the Bank because though the figures may be available in accounts but the impact of the grant of amounts to persons without proper credit will be actually felt when recovery steps start in due course.

Where a branch manager attempted to raise loan under SEEUY scheme in the name of his wife but did not encash the loan cheque, it was held that non-encashing does not matter and punishment from removal service was awarded.[2] Similarly, where branch manager took ₹ 25,000/- due to surgical operation of his wife unauthorisedly but later money was deposited back with 24% interest in Bank, the punishment of removal was upheld.[3]

It is immaterial whether any loss has been caused to the Bank. Supreme Court in the case of Nikunj Bihari Patnayak[4] has held

*"Even though no loss has been caused to Central Bank of India even then acting beyond one's authority is by itself a breach of discipline and breach of Regulation 3 which constitutes misconduct within the meaning of Regulation 24."*

Manner of Disciplinary Action/Proceedings to be drawn is generally given in further Regulations differing from Bank to Bank.

Similarly, where charges depict that Delinquent Officer tried to defraud Bank for his personal gain and in fact succeeded in his design, it is immaterial as to whether the Bank has suffered any financial loss or not because Bank having lost confidence in the Delinquent Officer cannot be found to be on fault.[5]

## False TA/Medical Bills etc.

It is the bounding duty of a responsible Bank Officer to make sure that any bill produced by him staking any claim for reimbursement from the Bank must be true and correct and it is the responsibility of the officer concerned to make sure that no incorrect claim is made to Bank. A Delinquent Officer in respect of TA bill took one of the defenses as under:

*".....please note that I have not certified anywhere in the TA bill that all the particulars furnished by me are true and correct. All bills are subject to normal errors, more so in the case of inspectors because they have to submit such bills frequently..."*

---

1. Biren Borah Vs United Bank of India & Others 2004 (2) Bank CLR 176 (Gau)
2. Ganesh Sunta Ram Sirur Vs Bank of India and Another 2005(1) Bank CLR 455 (S.C.)
3. Damoh Panna Sagar Regional Rural Bank and Another Vs Munnalal Jain 2005(1) Bank CLR 749 (S.C.)
4. Disciplinary Authority cum Regional Manager and Others Vs Nikunj Bihari Patnayak 1996(9) S.C.C. 69, Judgment Today 1996(4) S.C. 457
5. Biren Borah Vs United Bank of India and Others 2004(2) Bank CLR 176 (Gau)

The defense was treated as an irresponsible defense[1] where the charge in respect of L.T.C. bill was as under:

1. You have taken advance of ₹ 1,300 on 20/02/1986 from Sakchi branch towards cost of railway tickets for onward journey from Tatanagar station to visit Jagannath Puri in order to avail L.T.C. facility but subsequently refunded the amount on 28/08/1987.
2. You had requested vide your application dt. nil addressed to the manager Sakchi branch and received ₹ 1,300 on 20/02/7986, the cost of first class railway tickets for onward journey from Tata Nagar station to Jagannath Puri in respect of four adults and two children but you did not actually undertake the said journey.

On the above allegations, the charge of temporary embezzlements of funds was not found to arise in view of the L.T.C. rules where it was provided that when an officer takes advance and goes not to submit bills within seven days from the date of resumption of duties is liable to be recovered a lump sum from the salary of the officer and accordingly inquiry was quashed.[2]

## Unauthorised Absence

The Bank being a public institution, the employees are required to observe strict discipline of punctuality, efficiency and honesty. It is not the fundamental right of employee to remain absent without prior permission and that too without any just reason. However, in exigencies, employees may not be in a position to inform immediately to his employer for attending his duties on account of sudden sickness or accident, but at the earliest opportunity, the employee is required to inform his employer about the causes of his absence and if he is not in a position to report for the duty he must sent his report of leave at the earliest opportunity.

An employee who does not bother about obtaining necessary permission for a pretty long time will be treated as having committed misconduct. Being misconduct, management can hold an enquiry and may even pass an order of termination for unauthorised absence.

Where the contract/standing order/service rules are silent, the management has power to deduct the wages for absence of duty. Whether the deduction from wages will be pro-rata for the period of absence only or for a longer period, will depend upon the particular facts of a matter. It is not enough that the employees attend the place of work; they must put in the work allotted to them. It is for the work and not for mere attendance that the wages are paid. If the employees do not work even as a protest on collective basis but comply with the formalities, like signing on register etc., the wages can be deducted. Deduction of wages can also be done in pursuance

---

1. M.C. Charati Vs Personnel Manager and Disciplinary Authority, Syndicate Bank 2001(2) Bank CLR 90 (Kant)
2. Apoourva Ranjan Sarkar Vs Bank of India 1995(2) Bank CLR 181 (Patna)

to concerned enactment such as 'Payment of Wages Act' which provides for wage cuts for the absence from duty subject to its applicability. Though strike may be a legal one and legitimate and therefore may not invite Disciplinary Action/Proceedings which an illegal strike may do so, be it misconduct. But regardless of the legality of strike, the employees are liable to loose wages for the period of strike. During the period of strike, the contract of employment continues but the employees withhold their labour. Consequently, they cannot expect to be paid.

In cases of mass strike, management need not to conduct disciplinary inquiry either on individual basis or on mass basis but still has requisite power for deduction of wages on pro-rata basis. But such pro-rata need not be necessarily only for the hours of strike. Thus, even employees strike only for four hours or any part of the day, the salary of employees can be deducted for the whole day.[1]

The same will apply in cases of 'go slow action' or 'pen down strikes'.

There is no doubt whenever an employee indulges in a misconduct such as deliberate refusal to work, the employer/management can take Disciplinary Action/ Proceedings against and impose on him penalty prescribed for it which will include some deduction of wages. However, when misconduct is not disputed but is on other hand admitted and is resorted to on a mass scale, there is no need to held any inquiry. Where employee did not attend Bank for casting their votes in Gram Panchayat elections while the day of voting was not declared as a holiday under Negotiable Instrument Act but only a State holiday; afterwards an explanation was called by Bank for unauthorised absence, the Court held that it was necessary for employee to avail any kind of leave/permission and accordingly the Court refused to quash the explanation.[2]

No misconduct, where wife of the Delinquent Officer got a loan from Bank without disclosing the relationship on the basis of pledge of gold ornaments and loan application form was having no column for the disclosure of the fact that applicant is related to Bank Employee and she was otherwise entitled for loan. It was held that in absence of any circular/rule for disclosing relationship, no case of misconduct is made out.[3]

In another matter on the charge of insubordination due to refusal by the Delinquent Officer to operate vault of currency chest, the Delinquent Officer took plea in his reply that he has no experience of opening and closing the vault and that he did all the works of claims department except opening and closing of vault it was found that there is no foundation for alleged misconduct.[4]

---

1. Swatantra Kumar Singh Vs Gorakhpur Kshetriya Gramin Bank and Others 2000(3) Bank CLR 30 (Allahabad)
2. R. Gopal Krishnan Nair and Another Vs State Bank of Travancore 1997(2) Bank CLR 302 (Kerala)
3. Satyendra Kumar Ghosh Vs State Bank of India 1995(1) Bank CLR 638 (Patna)
4. Reserve Bank of India and Another Vs C.L. Toora and Others 2004(2) Bank CLR 323(S.C.)

In a case where the employee did not join duty within thirty days of the notice nor did he try to satisfy the Bank that he intended to join duty and he did not show any sincerity in joining duty in spite of leave not being granted, he even withdraw his leave applications, it was held that the condition necessary to deem a voluntary resignation satisfied and it was not to be interfered under Article. 227 of the Constitution and the writ petition was dismissed.[1]

Apart from the misconducts, as referred above, there are some other types of misconducts also. While the above referred misconducts arise out directly from Banking activity and decision as to committing of misconduct is taken by Bank authorities or their administrative heads.

Here, we intend to refer the misconducts which are indicated by other authorities like Courts or other statutory authorities. Instantly, we may refer the provisions of Right to Information Act wherein express power has been conferred upon the Information Commissioners to recommend for disciplinary action.

Going further, High Court, Supreme Court and other authorities also sometimes recommend for initiation of disciplinary action/proceedings against the erring officer. Such orders/references should be construed strictly. Beyond the specific language used in the statute or order, any action of management will be in violation of rules of natural justice.

1. T. Venkateswarlu Vs Branch Manager, State Bank of India, Vijaywada and Anr., 1990(1) Bank CLR 96 (H.C. A.P.)

# CHAPTER 2

# NATURE OF DISCIPLINARY ACTION/PROCEEDINGS

1. **Nature of Inquiry in Relation to Inquiry under Bipartite Settlement (a) Misconduct, (b) Penalties, (c) Offences, (d) Dispensing with Inquiry, (e) Records of Inquiry Proceedings**
2. **Criminal Proceedings and Disciplinary Action/Proceedings**
3. **Promotion and Disciplinary Action/Proceedings (Sealed Cover Procedure)**
4. **Retirement and Disciplinary Action/Proceedings after Retirement**

---

The Disciplinary Action/Proceedings are meant not really to punish the guilty but to keep the administrative machinery unsullied by getting rid of bad element. The interest of the Delinquent Officer also lies in a prompt conclusion of the Disciplinary Action/Proceedings. If he is not guilty of charges, his honour should be vindicated at the earliest possible moment and if he is guilty he should be dealt with promptly according to law and rules.

The purpose of Disciplinary Action/Proceedings is only to help the Disciplinary Authority to come to a conclusion regarding the misconduct of an employee.

The object of Disciplinary Action/Proceedings is to enable the management to hold an investigation into the charges framed against a Delinquent Officer so that management may in due course consider the evidence adduced and decide whether the charges are proved or not.

A departmental proceeding is a quasi-judicial proceeding. The Inquiring Authority performs a quasi-judicial function. The charges leveled against the Delinquent Officer must be found to have been proved. The Inquiring Authority has a duty to arrive at finding upon taking into consideration the materials brought on record by the parties.

The purported evidence collected during investigation by the Investigating Officer against all the accused by itself could not be treated to be evidence in the disciplinary proceeding.

Although the provisions of the Evidence Act are not applicable in the said proceeding, principles of natural justice are required to be complied with.

Inference of facts must be based on evidence which meet the requirements of legal principles.

If after setting aside the inquiry Court directs for fresh inquiry, it is clear that Inquiring Authority will apply his mind to the evidence on record comprising the examination-in-chief and cross-examination of the Bank witness as well as the Delinquent Officer's witness and therefore when even after order for fresh inquiry the Inquiring Authority submitted "Additional Inquiry Report", it was held that there has been no application of mind particularly in view of statement made by the Inquiring Authority that "the findings of the previous inquiry report remain as they are" and accordingly the second inquiry was also set aside.[1]

## 1. NATURE OF DISCIPLINARY ACTION PROCEEDINGS IN RELATION TO INQUIRY UNDER BIPARTITE SETTLEMENT

Under the present system of banking industry, the disciplinary action procedure is prescribed cadre wise. Sources prescribing the disciplinary action systems are different for officers and award staff of Bank. Though there are many similarities in both the systems and both aim towards finding the truth, yet there exists fundamental difference between the two systems. Practically speaking, officers and award staff perform different types of duties. Simultaneously, their authority and responsibility also differs while discharging their duties. In coming paragraphs, an effort has been made to chalk out the points of differentiation between above two types of disciplinary action.

### (a) Misconduct

In case of officers, there has been made no differentiation between gross misconduct and minor misconduct. A breach of any of the conduct regulations is considered to constitute misconduct. Conduct Regulations of Banks contain no list differentiating gross and minor misconduct. Whereas workman staff lists of gross and minor misconduct have been specially stated in the Bipartite Settlement.

---

1. Heera Prasad Vs State Bank of India and Others 1993(1) Bank CLR 674 (S.C.)

## (b) Penalties

For officers, list of major and minor penalties have been given. The penalties under the officer employee regulations are more severe than the penalties for workmen staff.

**(i) Major penalties:** The major penalties prescribed under the Regulations are reduction to a lower stage in a time scale, compulsory retirement, and removal from service and dismissal. There is no provision for a warning or censure or a fine or stoppage of increment or condonation of misconduct.

**(ii) Minor penalties:** The minor penalties prescribed apart from censure are withholding of increments of pay with or without cumulative effect, withholding the promotion and recovery from pay or such other amount as may be due to the officer of the whole or part of any pecuniary loss caused to the Bank by negligence or breach of orders.

On the other hand, penalties in case of workmen are less severe as compared to penalties of officers. As per Bipartite Settlement, an employee found guilty of gross misconduct apart from being dismissed may be warned or censured or have an adverse remark entered against him or be fined or have his increments stopped or have his misconduct condoned and merely be discharged.

As per Bipartite Settlement, an employee found guilty of minor misconduct may be warned or censured or have an adverse remark entered against him or have his increment stopped for a period not longer than six months.

## (c) Offences

So far as officers are concerned, no precise definition has been given in Conduct Regulations. On the other hand, as per Bipartite Settlement, offence means any offence involving moral turpitude for which an employee is liable to conviction and sentence under any provision of law.

**Suspension**

An officer may be placed under suspension where a Disciplinary Proceeding against him is contemplated or is pending. He may be suspended where a case against him in respect of any criminal offence is under investigation inquiry or trial.

In case of workmen, he may be suspended pending an inquiry or initiation of an inquiry in respect of a proposed disciplinary action against him. Workmen may be suspended as soon as the Proceedings against him are started.

**Charge-sheet**

In case of officers, where the proceedings have been instituted for major penalties, the charge-sheet shall contain definite and distinct charges on the basis of allegation and shall also contain the articles of charges together with a statement of allegations. In case of minor penalties, the charge-sheet shall contain imputation of lapses. Whereas, there is no prescribed format of charge-sheet as per Bipartite Settlement. The employee has to be given a charge-sheet clearly setting forth circumstances appearing against him.

**Service of Charge-sheet, Orders and Notices etc.**

As per Service Regulations, every order, notice and other process made or issued under the Regulations shall be served **in person** on the officer employee. There is no provision regarding deeming it to be good service.

Charge-sheet, orders, notices etc. can be communicated to an officer employee by registered post at his last known address. Again there is no provision when such communication shall be deemed to be a good service.

In case of workman, if an employee refuses to accept any notice, order, charge-sheet, written communication or written intimation in connection with Disciplinary Proceedings when it is sought to be served upon him, provided such refusal takes place in the presence of two witnesses including the person who goes to effect service upon him.

Further, in case of workman, where any notice, order, charge-sheet, intimation or any other official communication is sent to him by registered post acknowledgment due at the last recorded address communicated in writing by the employee and acknowledged by the Bank, the same will be deemed to be a good service.

**Time for Submission of Reply to Charge-sheet**

Time for replying to the charge-sheet shall not exceed 15 days but it may be extended by the Disciplinary Authority, whereas no time has been prescribed under Bipartite Settlement for replying to Charge-sheet. Normally, a reasonable time extending to about 3 to 7 days is given.

## (d) Dispensing with Inquiry

As far officer employee is concerned, no inquiry is necessary in case of minor penalty but inquiry as per procedure laid down in Regulations must be conducted before imposing major penalty.

As far workman is concerned, an inquiry need not be held if the employee is charged with minor misconduct and proposed punishment is warning or censure. Further, inquiry shall be conducted if proposed punishment more than warning or censure unless guilt is voluntarily admitted or when inquiry is not held on two previous occasions in respect of a minor misconduct.

An inquiry need not be held if the misconduct is such that even if proved, Bank does not intend to award the punishment of discharge or dismissal and the employee makes a voluntary admission of his guilt.

## (e) Records of Inquiry Proceedings

As far officers are concerned, no procedure has been outlined in Regulations, regarding maintaining the record of inquiry proceedings. However, it is advisable to keep the record. On the other hand, as per Bipartite Settlement, the inquiry proceedings should be entered in a book kept especially for the purpose. Further, the method of keeping such record in the register has been outlined in para 19.10 of the First Bipartite Settlement.

## Presenting Officer

There is specific provision in Conduct Regulations for appointment of Presenting Officer. In case of an officer, it is open to Disciplinary Authority to appoint even an outsider who is a 'public servant' as the Presenting Officer to present on its behalf the case in support of the articles of charges, whereas, there is no such provision in the Bipartite Settlement. However, normally, an officer of the Bank is appointed as Presenting Officer to present the Bank's case before the Inquiry Officer. Further, in case of workman staff, Bank cannot appoint outsider as Presenting Officer.

## Representation at the Inquiry

The officer employee may take the assistance of any other officer employee. But officer employee should be of the same Bank where the employee proceeded against is employed.

An officer may not engage a legal practitioner for the purpose of assistance, unless Presenting Officer appointed by the Disciplinary Authority is a legal practitioner or the Disciplinary Authority having regard to the circumstances of the case so permits. The officer employee cannot take the assistance of any other officer who has two pending Disciplinary cases in hand in which he has to give assistance.

On the other hand, a workman may be defended by a representative of a registered trade union of Bank employees or at the request of the said union by a representative of the Federation or All India Organisation to which such union is affiliated. The defense representative can be an outsider also.

## First Sitting at the Inquiry

If the officer employee does not plead guilty at the first sitting of the Inquiry, the Inquiring Authority shall adjourn the case to a later date not exceeding 30 days or within such extended time as may be granted by the Inquiring Authority. On the other hand, Bipartite Settlements do not provide for adjournment of Inquiry if the employee does not plead guilty on the first sitting. Inquiry may start right from the first day of Inquiry itself.

## Special Leave and TA, DA to Defense Representative

In case of officers, there is no provision regarding grant of special leave and payment of TA and DA to officer assisting the charge-sheeted employee. However, normally, these should be granted. Whereas, in case of workman staff, if the Defense Representative defending the employee is an employee of the same Bank at an outstation branch within same state, he shall be relieved on special leave (full pay and allowances) to represent the employee and be paid one to and fro fare.

## Joint and Common Inquiry

As per Officers' Conduct Regulations where two or more officers are concerned in a case, the authority competent to impose a major penalty on all such officers may make proceedings against all of them may be taken in a common proceeding.

As far workman staff is concerned, there is no specific provision under the Bipartite Settlement but in cases where there are same charges and in respect of same incident, normally joint inquiry is conducted.

**Written Briefs/Arguments**

In case of officers, the Inquiring Authority may hear the Presenting Officer and the officer after the completion of the production of evidence or permit them to file written briefs of their respective cases within 15 days of the completion of production of evidence. Whereas in case of workman staff, there is no specific provision for submission of brief/arguments. However, normally, an opportunity is provided to submit written/arguments.

**Inquiring Authority Report**

Officers' Conduct Regulations provide that the Inquiring Authority report shall contain:

(i) A gist of articles of charges and statements of imputation of misconduct or misbehaviour;

(ii) A gist of evidence of the officer in respect of each article of charge;

(iii) An assessment of evidence in respect of each article of charge;

(iv) The finding on each article of charge and the reasons thereof.

As far workman staff is concerned, no specific format has been prescribed for Inquiry Officer's report.

**Submission of the Report**

Officers' Service Regulations provide that Inquiring Authority shall forward to the Disciplinary Authority, the following:

(i) The Report;

(ii) The written statement of defense, if any, submitted by the officer;

(iii) The oral and documentary evidence produced in the course of inquiry;

(iv) Written briefs submitted by parties, if any;

(v) Orders, if any, made by the Disciplinary Authority and the Inquiry Officer in regard to the inquiry.

Whereas, there is no provision under the Bipartite Settlement regarding the documents etc. to be sent alongwith the report.

The procedure for imposing of penalties in case of Officer staff does not provide for a second opportunity to show cause against proposed punishment. On the other hand, as per Bipartite Settlement, a workman shall be given a hearing as regards the nature of the proposed punishment in case any charge is established against him.

**Second Inquiry**

In case of officers, the Disciplinary Authority can remit the case to the Inquiring Authority for fresh or further inquiry. Whereas there is no specific provision in this regard in case of workman staff. However, it is within the right of the Disciplinary Authority to order for a further inquiry.

**Number of Penalties/Punishment**

In case of officers, there is no restriction regarding one penalty for one charge. Officers' Conduct Regulations provide the minor and major penalties which may be imposed on an officer. Whereas, as per Bipartite Settlement, a workman found guilty of misconduct, whether gross or minor shall not be given more than one punishment in respect of any one charge.

**Appeal After Inquiry**

Officers can appeal against an order imposing upon him any of the penalties within 45 days from the date of receipt of the order in accordance with Conduct Regulations.

In the same way, workman can also appeal against orders passed in disciplinary matters within 45 days from the date on which the original order has been communicated in writing to the employee concerned in accordance with Bipartite Settlement.

**Powers of the Appellate Authority**

In case of officers, the Appellate Authority can confirm, enhance, and reduce the said penalty. On the other hand, in case of workman staff, the Appellate Authority has no right to enhance punishment in the appeal under any circumstances.

**Hearing by Appellate Authority**

In case of officers, there is no provision for hearing by Appellate Authority before disposing of appeal, even in case of dismissal unless penalty is to be enhanced. In case of workman staff, as per Bipartite Settlement, in a case of dismissal, if the employee desires, Appellate Authority should hear him or his representative before disposing of the appeal.

**Time for Disposal of Appeal**

As far officers are concerned, there has been provided no time specifically for disposal of appeal. Whereas in case of workman staff, where hearings are not required an appeal shall be disposed of within two months from the date thereof. In other cases, it shall be disposed of within one month from the date of conclusion of hearings.

**Review**

In case of officers, the Reviewing Authority may review a case within six months of the final order and can pass orders as it may deem fit, whereas in case of workman staff there is no such provision.

**Consultation with C.V.C.**

In case of officers, in cases having vigilance angle particularly in respect of scale III and above, Bank has to consult C.V.C. On the other hand, there is no such provision in case of workman staff.

## 2. CRIMINAL PROCEEDINGS AND DISCIPLINARY ACTION/PROCEEDINGS

Often in cases where criminal case against the Delinquent Officer is either pending or has been started and simultaneously management decides to carry on the inquiry/DAP, an objection is raised that in view of criminal case the management cannot and should not proceed for in-house proceedings.

Firstly, we will discuss the scope of both the proceedings. The approach and the objective of criminal case are quite distinct and different. Comparing the two Disciplinary Action/Proceedings, the basic question is whether the Delinquent Officer is guilty of such conduct as will warrant his removal from service or a lesser punishment whereas in criminal case the question is whether the offences registered under Prevention of Corruption Act or Indian Penal Code are proved and if proved what sentence to be imposed upon. In other words, a criminal prosecution is launched for an offence or violation of duty which the Delinquent Officer caused to the society. Omission of public duty and violation of law is inherent in a crime while the discipline in service and efficiency in public service is to be examined under Disciplinary Action/ Proceedings. There is no question of an offence or an act of omission being punishable in law to be investigated under Disciplinary Action/Proceedings. There is no possibility of imposing a punishment decided by law which makes that act or omission an offence in Disciplinary Action/Proceedings.

The standard of proof, the mode of inquiry and rules governing the inquiry and trial of a criminal case are entirely different. In criminal case, the charge must be proved beyond reasonable shadow of doubt while in Disciplinary Action/Proceedings the proof required is that of preponderance of probability. Preponderance of probability is the test *vis-à-vis* human conduct. *The Inquiring Authority can reach to a different conclusion than that arrived at in a criminal case.* It is immaterial whether the charges are identical or the witnesses were the same as long as the power exercised by the Court and the inquiry under the relevant service law are distinct and separate.

So far as stay of Disciplinary Action/Proceedings is concerned, the general rule is that pendency of a criminal case will not impede the authority to conduct the inquiry or to wait the conclusion of the trial for offences thereof without pursuing the remedies under Disciplinary Action/Proceedings. Merely because proceedings in criminal case are in Court there is no prohibition for the Disciplinary Authority to conduct the inquiry and to complete the same and to award punishment. Merely because the same set of facts constitute the fundamentals in action under Disciplinary Action/Proceedings are also subject-matter in trial before Court, the management is not prevented to carry out Disciplinary Action/Proceedings for the misconduct committed by the Delinquent Officer.

Yet under certain circumstances, simultaneous proceedings may not be desirable or appropriate. Grounds for stay of Disciplinary Action/Proceedings may be that the defense of the Delinquent Officer in the criminal case may be/will be prejudiced or the case is of serious nature involving questions of law and facts which are not simple and therefore advisable to await the decision of criminal case. However, no hard and fast rule can be laid down.

However, Supreme Court[1] has explained the law on the subject as under in para 7 and 8 of the referred ruling—

*"7. The view expressed in the three cases of this Court seem to support the position that while there could be no legal bar for simultaneous proceedings being taken, yet, there may be cases where it would be appropriate to defer Disciplinary Action/Proceedings awaiting disposal of the criminal case. In the latter class of cases, it would be open to the Delinquent Officer employee to seek such an order of stay or injunction from the Court. Whether in the facts and circumstances of a particular case there should or should not be such simultaneity of the proceedings would then receive judicial consideration and the Court will decide in the given circumstances of a particular case as to whether the Disciplinary Action/Proceedings should be interdicted, pending criminal trial. As we already stated that it is neither possible nor advisable to evolve a hard and fast, straight jacket formula valid for all cases and of general application without regard to the particularities of the individual situation. For the disposal of the present case, we do not think it necessary to say anything more, particularly when we do not intend to lay down any general guideline.*

*8. In the instant case, the criminal action and the Disciplinary Action/ Proceedings are grounded upon the same set of facts. We are of the view that the Disciplinary Action/Proceedings should have been stayed and the High Court was not right in interfering with the trial Court's order of injunction which had been affirmed in appeal."*

Thus, advisability, desirability of Disciplinary Action/Proceedings can be determined in each case taking into account all the facts and circumstances of a peculiar case. Delay in criminal case may itself be a good ground for going ahead with the Disciplinary Action/Proceedings even where Disciplinary Action/Proceedings are stayed at an earlier stage. When an employee without submitting his explanation to the charge-sheet rushed to Court Supreme Court held[2] firstly, the Authority in department is the appropriate authority to consider whether it is worthwhile or not to await the decision of Criminal Court and in absence of his explanation it cannot be said how his defense will be prejudice. Otherwise also the trial of a criminal case may get prolonged by the dilatory method used by a Delinquent Officer. The Delinquent Officer cannot be permitted to on one hand prolong criminal case and at the same time contend that Disciplinary Action/Proceedings should be stayed due to pendency of criminal case.[3]

---

1. Kusheshwari Dubey Vs M/S Bharat Cooking Coal Ltd. 1988(4) S.C.C. 319
2. Abhai Raj Singh Vs Bank of Baroda 2005(3) Bank CLR 70 (All)
3. State Bank of India and Others Vs R.B. Sharma 2004(2) Bank CLR 571 (S.C.)

Article 20(2) of the Constitution of India runs as under—

*"No person shall be prosecuted and punished for the same offence more than once."*

Section 300 of Cr PC also bars a second trial for the same offence when a Court of competent jurisdiction has already convicted or acquitted a person for the same offence. The principle embodied in Article 20(2) and Section 300 Cr PC is based on the maxim *'memobis vexati debet pro eadem caesa'*. If some allegations are made against a person and he is tried in respect of those allegations and he is either acquitted or convicted, he should not be tried again with respect to the offences based on the same allegations.

However, the prosecution contemplated under Article 20(2) must be in relation to the law which creates the offence and the punishment must also be in accordance with what the law prescribes. In case of Disciplinary Action/Proceedings, the question of *double jeopardy* does not rise because charge under Disciplinary Action/ Proceedings is not an offence under the Criminal Procedure Code and therefore, Article 20 of the Constitution is of little assistance. It is no doubt true that the accused is entitled to keep mum when the trial in the criminal court is going on and the burden is on the prosecution to establish the case beyond all reasonable doubt. But the same will be the case in the enquiry into misconduct in a disciplinary proceeding. It is always for the management, in the first instance to establish its case and it is for the Delinquent Officer to rebut the case. The presenting officer on behalf of the disciplinary authority has to prove the misconduct against the Delinquent Officer. Therefore, it is for the Delinquent Officer to take up his stand. Merely because criminal cases are pending, it cannot prevent him from participating in the Disciplinary Action/Proceedings.[1]

Supreme Court has further clarified, if there are additional charges against the Delinquent Officer which was not the subject-matter of allegations in criminal case, the Disciplinary Action/Proceedings cannot be stayed.[2]

If an employee is acquitted of criminal charge, the same by itself will not be a ground not to initiate departmental proceedings against him and to drop the same in the event an order of acquittal is passed. As acquittal in the criminal case is not determinative of the commission of misconduct or otherwise and it is open to the authorities to proceed with the Disciplinary Action/Proceedings notwithstanding acquittal in criminal case. Acquittal *per se* does not entitle the employee to claim immunity from the proceedings at the most factum of acquittal may be a circumstance to be considered while awarding punishment.

It will depend upon facts of each case and even that cannot have universal application.[3] Therefore, when a Disciplinary Action/Proceedings is initiated after a

---

1. M. Rama Rao Vs Regional Manager, State Bank of India 1989(2) Bank CLR 414
2. Indian Overseas Bank Anna Salai and Another Vs P. Ganeshan and Others 2008(2) Bank CLR 597 (S.C.)
3. Chairman and Managing Director, United Commercial Bank and Others Vs P.C. Kakkar 2003(1) Bank CLR 622 (S.C.)

gap of seven years on the self same facts which were under judicial trial and the Delinquent Officer was acquitted, it will be unjust and unfair to record contrary findings in Disciplinary Action/Proceedings on the self same facts particularly when judicial pronouncement has been made after a regular hearing.[1]

Further, confidential statement made by accused in criminal trial would not be a bar to proceed in departmental enquiry.[2]

Where the Delinquent Officer was guilty of misappropriation and made admission of guilt before Bank authorities and paid misappropriated amount in five installments the case was not found fit for stay of Disciplinary Action/Proceedings.[3] However, where employee was exonerated in criminal case and while criminal case and Disciplinary Action/Proceedings were on the same set of facts, it was held that the distinction which is usually drawn as between the Disciplinary Action/Proceedings and criminal case on the basis of approach and burden of proof will not be applicable and therefore the Disciplinary Action/Proceedings/order will be liable to be quashed.[4]

And any order of acquittal in criminal case finding, the Delinquent Officer not guilty of misappropriation/deriving personal benefit and causing loss to the Bank will be liable to be noticed by Bank authorities.[5] Lastly, if a Delinquent Officer has been acquitted of criminal charges, the same neither can be ground not to initiate Disciplinary Action/Proceedings against him nor to drop the same if pending.[6]

## 3. PROMOTION AND DISCIPLINARY ACTION/ PROCEEDINGS (SEALED COVER PROCEDURE)

Bank management is entitled to lay down policy decision fixing the criteria for grant of promotion. The eligibility norms for promotions are defined by Bank on a realistic basis wherefor a system to choose the best available talent. Changes in such policy are required to be made keeping in view the requirement as also the exigency of the situation prevailing at the relevant time. The sealed cover procedure is now a well established concept in service jurisprudence. The procedure is adopted when an employee is due for promotion, increment etc., but Disciplinary/Criminal proceedings are pending against him or have been ordered and hence the findings as to his entitlement to the service benefit of promotion/increment are kept in a sealed cover to be opened after proceedings in question are over. If any penalty is imposed upon on the Delinquent Officer as a result of Disciplinary Action/Proceedings or if he is found guilty in Court proceedings, the findings in sealed cover/covers are not acted upon.

---

1. Bhimsen Gochhayat Vs Regional Manager, Bank of India and Others 2007(2) Bank CLR 392 (Orissa)
2. Commissioner of Police, New Delhi Vs Narendra Singh 2006(4) S.C.C. 265
3. Al-Chidambaram Vs Indian Overseas Bank Mumbai 1997(2) Bank CLR 605 (Madras)
4. Dr. Prasanna Kumar Agrawal Vs State Bank of India and Others 2002(2) Bank CLR 549 (Gau)
5. Managing Director, State Bank of Hyderabad and Another Vs P. Kata Rao 2009(1) Bank CLR 199 (S.C.)
6. Commissioner of Police, New Delhi Vs Narendra Singh 2006(4) S.C.C. 265

Thus, promotion of the Delinquent Officer will be considered in usual course.

Pendency of preliminary investigation will not attract '**sealed cover procedure**' and it can be applied only on the conclusion of preliminary investigation where Departmental Authority has formed its opinion and has passed an order of the effect that the officer is to be charge-sheeted for departmental action.

In absence of any such order, the officer will be treated similarly with other officers in matter of consideration of promotion.

Thus, where in a case charges are under investigation and a member of staff is otherwise found suitable for promotion, his promotion will be released. However, he may be informed of the effect in case of need that in case punishment is awarded on conclusion of Disciplinary Action/Proceedings, the same will be inflected in the grade/scale staff is working at the time of awarding punishment.

The officer cannot be rewarded with promotion as a matter of course even if the penalty is other than the reduction in rank. Virtually, an employee has no right for promotion but has only a right to be considered for promotion. To qualify for promotion, the least that is expected of an employee is to have an unblemished record. An employee found guilty of misconduct cannot be placed at par with the other employees. When an officer is held guilty and penalised and is, therefore not promoted at least till the date on which he is penalised, he cannot be said to have been subjected to a further penalty on that account. The denial of promotion is not a penalty but a necessary consequence of his conduct. Therefore, while considering an employee for promotion, his whole record is to be taken into consideration and if promotion committee takes the penalties imposed upon the employee into consideration and denies for the promotion such denial will be neither unjustified nor illegal. Though Supreme Court[1] has laid down that it is only when a charge-memo/charge-sheet in a Disciplinary Action/Proceeding or framing of charge in criminal prosecution is made it can be said that Disciplinary Action/Proceedings. Criminal Proceedings are pending yet in case where Conduct Regulations of Bank speak otherwise the same will prevail.

Thus, when Promotion Committee holds its proceedings at a stage where no inquiry is pending; the sealed cover procedure cannot be resorted to and any punishment awarded in Disciplinary Action/Proceedings which started in later years and punishment made cannot deprive the Delinquent Officer of the benefit of promotion earned before initiation of Disciplinary Action/Proceedings.[2]

However, in this connection, the ultimate position will be decided in accordance with the circulars of Bank which generally lay down what procedure will be applicable to promotions. Generally, in the following cases, the sealed cover procedure can be adopted—

---

1. Union of India and Others Vs K.V. Janki Raman and Others 1991(4) S.C.C. 109
2. Bank of India and Another Vs Degala Suryanarayana 1999(2) Bank CLR 313 S.C.

1. Officers against whom Disciplinary Action/Proceedings have been ordered.
2. Where a *prima facie* disciplinary case is in existence in the view of Disciplinary Authority and an order of this effect has been passed.
3. Officers against whom Disciplinary Action/Proceedings are pending.
4. Where prosecution has been registered in Court of law or criminal case is pending.
5. Officers who are under suspension.

## 4. RETIREMENT AND DISCIPLINARY ACTION/ PROCEEDINGS AFTER RETIREMENT

The age of retirement of officers and other staff of the various Banks established in India has been subject-matter of several awards and settlements from several years but upon nationalisation of banks' rationalisation in the age of retirement has been made.

It is noticeable that Disciplinary Action/Proceedings are initiated only when a charge-sheet is issued. Pendency of any preliminary inquiry therefore by itself will not be and cannot be a ground for invoking the relevant provision of Service Regulation. Sometimes, Bank decides to initiate Disciplinary Action/Proceedings at the fag-end of one's career. In Service Regulations, *a legal fiction is created wherein a right is given to Bank to continue with Disciplinary Action/Proceedings as if the employee is in service until its conclusion and final order is passed. The scope and ambit of such legal fiction will be confined to object and purport for which the same has been created. Such provision will apply only when the Disciplinary Action/ Proceedings had clearly been initiated prior to the employee ceases to be in service.*[1] A domestic enquiry after retirement would not be a 'disciplinary inquiry' within the ordinary meaning of the term but an inquiry confined to the purpose of rules, viz., whether the employee should be granted any pensionary benefits, and if so, to what extent such an inquiry can also be made after the retirement on attaining the age of superannuating. If there is sufficient material disclosing grave irregularities on the part of the employee, the bank will be well within its powers in refusing to sanction pensionary benefits, or in sanctioning them only partly.

Service Regulations provide that an employee shall retire on attaining the age of 58/60 years but there is nothing in Service Regulations to pass any order by management. Retirement is automatic. Employee need not to wait for an order from Bank once he attains the age of 58/60 years.

Therefore, where an officer retired on attaining superannuation and no order extending service was served on him for pending Disciplinary Action/Proceedings. before retirement any order of suspension will loose all its effect and similarly any dismissal order passed after retirement will be null and void.[2] Later on, Supreme

1. UCO Bank Vs Rajinder Lal Kapoor 2007(3) Bank CLR 31 (S.C.)
2. P.S. Balasubramanian Vs The Chief General Manager, State Bank of India 1991(1) Bank CLR 233

Court[1] took a different view in relation to Punjab National Bank officer employee (Discipline of Appeal) Regulation 1977 that it may be true that the question of imposition of dismissal of the Delinquent Officer from service when he has already reached the age of superannuation would not ordinarily arise. However, as the consequences of such an order is provided for in service rule, imposition of such a punishment would not be wholly impermissible in law and further clarified that in case of dismissal service of the Delinquent Officer cannot be qualified for pensionary benefits.

Where an employee was dismissed just before retirement in Disciplinary Action Proceedings and which order of dismissal was set aside in Court and departmental Appellate Authority was directed for taking decision as to legality and validity of punishment, the Disciplinary Action/Proceedings were treated as pending after retirement and liable to be taken to its logical end.[2]

Where certain charges are leveled and the employee reverted to lower post but on the orders of High Court reinstated after finding inquiry improper and illegal. A fresh inquiry was started on the same charges and again reverted. Supreme Court held that earlier order was quashed on technical ground, therefore on merits, second inquiry can be held.

1. Ramesh Chandra Sharma Vs Punjab National Bank and Another 2008(1) Bank CLR 645 (S.C.)
2. Venkatarama Murlidhar Shenoy Vs Syndicate Bank 2001(2) Bank CLR 48 (Calcutta)
3. Anand Narain Shukla Vs State of M.P. 1979(39) FLR 325 (S.C.)

# CHAPTER 3

# APPLICATION OF PRINCIPLES OF NATURAL JUSTICE

The right of being heard though not a fundamental right, is a fundamental principle for judging fairness in action. Though no codified canons, yet they are the principles ingrained into the conscience of man. It is substance of justice which has to determine its form. The expression 'natural justice' and 'legal justice' do not present a watertight classification. Natural justice relieves legal justice from unnecessary technicalities, grammatical pedantry or logical prevarication. It supplies the omission of a formulated law. The first and foremost principle is 'no one should be condemned unheard'. Notice is the first limb of this principle. Notice should be clear. Notice should apprise the Delinquent Officer determinatively the case he has to meet with. Time given for the purpose must be adequate so as to make one enable to make his defense. In absence of a notice and consequent reasonable opportunity, the order passed becomes wholly vitiated. Thus, it is but essential that a party should be put on notice of the case before any adverse order is passed against him. Principles of natural justice are those rules which have been laid down by the Courts as being the minimum protection of the rights of an individual against the arbitrary procedure that may be adopted by a judicial, quasi-judicial and administrative authority while making an order affecting those rights. These rules are intended to prevent such authority from doing injustice.

The expression 'natural justice' implies justice according to conscience meaning thereby that while deciding an issue one will be guided by his own conscience with reference to the facts available before him. The aim of tool of principles of natural justice is to secure justice or to put it negatively to prevent miscarriage of justice.

Stating it broadly and without intending it to be exhaustive, it may be said that principles of natural justice require that a party should have the opportunity of adducing all relevant evidence on which he relies, that the evidence of the opponent should be taken in his presence and that he should be given the opportunity of cross-examining the witnesses, examined by that party and that no material should be relied upon against him without him being given an opportunity to explain such evidence.

The principles of 'natural justice' have taken deep roots in administration and in judicial system of the country. They are implicit in every decision whatever may be nature of decision, administrative, judicial or quasi-judicial. Even if rule or statute is silent about the observance of the principles of 'natural justice', such silence has been treated to imply compliance of the principle of natural justice. No form or procedure should ever be permitted to exclude the presentation of a litigant's defense or stand. Even where the statute is silent about the observance of principles of 'natural justice', such statutory silence is taken to imply compliance with the rules of 'natural justice' where substantial rights to parties are considerably affected.

The expression '**natural justice**' is comprised of two words, one is '**natural**' and other is **'justice'**. The word 'natural justice' is the derivative of the word 'nature' which literally means the basic or inherent features, tendencies, qualities or character of a person or thing. It also relates to the inborn or hereditary characteristic which influence or determine a fair personality of a human being influenced by the unfair worldly affairs.

The second word 'justice' is a derivation of the word 'just' which means upright, fair or proper. As such, the expression '**natural justice**' would mean the upright, fair or proper decisions or propositions or authorities worthy of being appreciated by the innate quality of human being of being fair, which guides the decisions.

The natural justice has been given various understanding. It is also understood as another name of common sense justice. Common sense in respect of the natural justice means the natural sense to distinguish what is right and what is wrong. Natural justice does not comprise in itself any technicality of justice and as such it comprises within its scope a fundamental quality of fairness without adapting which the justice could not appear to be done. The soul of natural justice is *'fair play in action'*. As such, natural justice is free from element of bias and provides equal opportunity for hearing the matter.

It is a concept of developing norms in their applicability to various aspects of social complicacies and technicalities to ensure fairness in actions and decisions.

Principles of natural justice are dynamic concept. It is now well established that they are not technical rules of justice and therefore unless prejudice is shown the application of principle of natural justice will be doubtful.

Over the years, there has been a considerable expansion of the principles of natural justice on the basis of various judicial dictums. Even in areas where there is no express statutory requirement of hearing, the requirements to such an extent as to hold that the principles of natural justice are an inbuilt content of Article 14 of the

Constitution and thus a fundamental requirement of any judicial/quasi-judicial system in India. They are flexible concept developed in order to provide real justice. Long back, Supreme Court held[1]

*"Natural justice is not unruly horse not lurking landmine nor a judicial cure-all. If fairness is shown by the decision-maker to the man proceeded against, the form, feature and fundamentals of such essential processual, propriety being conditioned by the facts and circumstances of each situation, no breach of natural justice can be complained of. Unnatural expansion of natural justice, without reference to the administrative reality and other factors of a given case can be exasperating. We can neither be finical nor fanatical but should be flexible yet firm in this jurisdiction."*

Courts have been consistent with the concept. The principles of natural justice are fundamental in the constitutional set-up of India. The concept has developing scope with the dynamic interpretation of Articles 14, 21, 311, of the Constitution etc. The various dimensions of the principles of natural justice are the principle of legitimate expectation, fair hearing, notice, right to information on facts relating to the dispute of, use of discretionary power and recording of reasons and their declaration.

The Courts have insisted on these. The shift now is to a broader notion of fairness or fair procedure in the administrative action. So far as management is concerned, the duty is not so much to act judicially as to act fairly. Supreme Court[2] again recognised the changing trend by holding that at one point of time breach of principles of natural justice was in itself treated as prejudice and that no other de-facto prejudice needed to be quote. But since then the rigor of the rule has been relaxed and now the principle is that in addition to breach of natural justice prejudice must also be proved and there is no such thing as a merely technical infringement of natural justice.

Though Disciplinary Action/Proceedings are administrative function which the law requires to be exercised in some respects as if it were judicial function, a quasi-judicial decision is also an administrative function which is subject to some measure of judicial procedure such as principles of natural justice. A judicial decision is made according to codified or uncodified law or statute while an administrative judgment is taken on the basis of policy. Quasi-judicial decision is a decision of administrative nature taken in a judicial manner in some respects.

The fundamental norms of natural justice are:

***Audi Alteram Partem*** — This maxim means to hear the other side; to hear both sides. In this rule, the opportunity of hearing must be given to the parties. The meaning of this maxim is of wider amplitude. It connotes that in litigation, the party must be given a fair opportunity of being heard, to controvert, to contradict or to correct anything prejudicial to its interest in the litigation.

The meaning of the maxim was explained in the observation of the Supreme Court[3] which reads as under:

---

1. Chairman Board of Mining Examination Vs Ramji 1977(34) F.L.R. 381 (S.C.)
2. M.C. Mehta Vs Union of India 1999(6) S.C.C. 237
3. Union of India Vs Tulsi Ram Patel, AIR 1985 SC 1416 at page 1460

*"Audi alteram partem rule, in its fullest amplitude, means that a person against whom an order to his prejudice may be passed should be informed of the allegations and charges against him, be given an opportunity of submitting his explanation thereto, have the right to know the evidence, both oral or documentary, by which the matter is proposed to be decided against him, and to inspect the documents which are relied upon for the purpose of being used against him, to have the witnesses who are to give evidence against him examined in his presence and have the right to cross-examine them, and to lead his own evidence, both oral and documentary, in his defense."*

***Nemo debet esse judex in propria sua causs* or Rule against BIAS** — This maxim means that no man can be judged in his own cause. The wider meaning of the maxim is that no one acting judicially should have or appear likely to have a bias in favour of one side or the other. The bias should not appear in the action of a judge. His mind should not be influenced by any love or hate. The justice must be routed in confidence and the factors which tilt the judge's confidence should not be allowed to influence or touch the judge's mind. The natural justice always condemns the bias in action and bias in doing justice. In Black's Law Dictionary, the term **'bias'** has been defined as under:

*"Condition of mind, which sways judgment and renders judge unable to exercise his functions impartially in particular case."*

Any type of leaning towards one side in a case for some reason beyond the reason which gives impetus to disposition of justice falls within the ambit of bias. The Supreme Court[1] may be quoted usefully in this regard:

*"But the application of principle of natural justice does not imply that what is not evidence can be acted upon. On the other hand, what it means is that no materials can be relied upon to establish a contested fact which are not spoken to by persons who are competent to speak about them and are subjected to cross-examination by the party against whom they are sought to be used.*

*When a document is produced in a Court or a Tribunal, the question that naturally arises is, is it a genuine document, what are its contents and are the statements contained therein true. When the appellant produced the balance sheet and profit and loss account of the company, it does not by its mere production amount to a proof of it or of the truth of the entries therein. If these entries are challenged, the appellant must prove each of such entries by producing the books and speaking from the entries made therein.*

*If a letter or other document is produced to establish some fact which is relevant to the enquiry, the writer must be produced or his affidavit in respect thereof be filed and opportunity afforded to the opposite party who challenges this fact. This is both in accord with principles of natural justice as also according to the producer under*

1. M/S Barelly Electric Supply Co. Ltd. Vs The Workmen and Others A.I.R. 1972 (S.C.) 30

*Order XIX Civil Procedure Code and the Evidence Act both of which incorporate these principles. Even if all technicalities of the Evidence Act are not strictly applicable except insofar as Section 11 of the Industrial Dispute Act, 1947 and the rules prescribed therein permit it, it is inconvincible that the Tribunal can act on what is not evidence such as hearsay, nor can it justify the Tribunal in basing it award on copies of documents when the originals which are in existence are not produced and proved by one of the methods either by affidavit or by witness who have executed them, if they are alive and can be produced."*

Bias may be generally described as a partiality or preference. 'Bias' is a preconceived opinion, predisposition or predetermination to decide a case or an issue in a particular manner, so much so that such predisposition does not leave the mind open to conviction. 'Bias' is a condition of mind which sways judgment and renders a judge unable to exercise impartiality in a particular case. To have a matter determined by an unbiased judge or a Tribunal is an extension, if not a part of the principles of natural justice. It is an elementary rule of natural justice that a person who tries a case should be able to deal with the matter before him objectively, fairly and impartially. The word impartially is the antonym of the word partiality or bias. A person trying case even quasi-judicial proceedings must not only act fairly but must be able to act above suspicion of unfairness. The onus of proving bias is on the person who alleges it. The colligation must be clearly proven if the proceedings are sought to be set aside. The apprehension has to be judged from healthy, reasonable and over all points of view and not on mere apprehension of a whimsical person.

Bias may take many forms. It may be pecuniary or non-pecuniary; personal or with regard to the subject-matter of the dispute; it may be political. Once conclusion is reached that an officer entrusted with the duty of deciding has entertained bias, he becomes disqualified to function as Inquiring Authority since discharge of such function by him will be opposed to all canons of fair play. The test is not whether the Authority has in reality become biased but whether the person who is to be affected by the decision has a reasonable ground to apprehend bias. Once the apprehension of bias is established, the function of reaching the decision must be negative to the Authority since the cardinal rule is that justice must not only be done but must appear to have been done. The only limitation is that the apprehension of bias is not the product of hallucination but is referable to such materials that a reasonable man placed under similar circumstances would develop an apprehension of bias. Thus, where a Delinquent Officer during pendency of inquiry being under suspension was thrown out of the quarter of the Bank, the factor was not considered as a proof of bias because the management's contention was that accommodation is to be made available to an employee who is on duty and working.[1]

Where the person issuing charge-sheet, show cause and rejecting the reply of employee later on becomes appellate authority and rejects the appeal of the employee,

---

1. Karuna Ketan Ganguly Vs Allahabad Bank 1997(1) Bank CLR 434 (Calcutta)

the official bias is likely to arise when an adjudicator has previous knowledge of the material facts of the case before him by virtue of his dealing with those facts in some other capacity. In such a case, the possibility of predispositions hovering over the mind of adjudicator for or against the part in the case before him cannot be ruled out. Accordingly, the order passed by such appellate authority was treated bad.[1]

It is an established view of law that where a party despite knowledge of the defect in the jurisdiction or bias or malice of an Inquiring Authority/arbitrator, participates in the proceedings without any kind of protest or objection by his conduct disentitles himself from raising such a question.

Appointment of an incompetent Inquiring Authority may not vitiate the entire proceedings.[2] A predisposition to decide for or against one party without proper regard to the true merits of the disputes is bias. The test for bias is whether a reasonable intelligent man fully apprised of the circumstances would face a serious apprehension of bias. Where a branch manager issued Demand Notice against one of the borrowers and the same was replied by borrower making allegation against the Zonal Manager and also filed a complaint before National Consumer Forum against Branch Manager as well as Zonal Manager and a common defense was taken before National Consumer Forum, the Zonal Manager in the capacity of Disciplinary Authority issued a show cause memo intending to initiate Disciplinary Action/Proceedings.

The apprehension of the Delinquent Officer was held justified that action against him is being taken only with a view to absolve Zonal Manager and accordingly Disciplinary Authority was changed by the Court.[3]

Whenever an inquiring authority becomes personally involved with one of the parties either management or the Delinquent Officer, suspicion that determination may not be exclusively on the merits of the case and the hearing in inquiry will arise which will disqualify the Inquiring Authority to act. Thus, cases of bias and ostensible bias had to be regarded in the light of their own circumstances and circumstances of one case will have no relevance to another case. The application of the Principle of Natural Justice to industrial employment is recognition of the expanding concept of social justice. Though the management of a Bank has the power to direct its own internal administration and discipline, the emergence of this concept has resulted in subjecting managerial discretion to certain rules.

From the analysis of the various judicial pronouncements and Indian Evidence Act, we may summarise the 'principles of natural justice' as follows:

(i) The Inquiring Authority is not permitted to collect any material from outside sources during the conduct of enquiry.

---

1. M. Sachidanandan Vs A.G.M. (Disciplinary Authority) and Others 1998(2) Bank CLR 155 (Karnataka)
2. H.V. Nirmala Vs Karnatak State Finance Corporation 2008(3) Bank CLR 63 (S.C.)
3. P.S. Karwade Vs UCO Bank and Others 1996(1) Bank CLR 495 (M.P.)

(ii) In a domestic enquiry, fairness in the procedure is a part of the principle of natural justice.

(iii) Exercise of discretionary power involve two elements: (a) Objective and (b) Subjective and existence of exercise of an objective element is a condition precedent for exercise of the subjective element.

(iv) It is not possible to lay down any rigid rules of the principle of natural justice which depends on the facts and circumstances of each case but the concept of fair play in action is the basis.

(v) The Inquiring Authority is not permitted to travel beyond the charges and any punishment imposed on the basis of a finding which was not the subject-matter of the charges is illegal. But in some banks, conduct rules permits that punishment can be awarded for a charge though not given in charge-sheet, but proved during the enquiry.

(vi) Suspicion or presumption cannot take the place of proof in a domestic enquiry.

(vii) Reasonable opportunity includes adequate and timely opportunities to the Delinquent Officer to prove his innocence and to lead his evidence in support of his side including any evidence in rebuttal to management's evidence.

(viii) Inquiring Authority must act in good faith and must not be interested otherwise on any account.

(ix) Punishment should always be proportionate to the charges proved. Excessive punishment is itself proof of bias.

The charges in departmental proceedings are not required to be proved like a criminal trial, i.e., beyond all reasonable doubts but Inquiring Authority upon a fair analysis of the documents must arrive at a conclusion that there had been a preponderance of probability to prove the charges on the basis of materials on record. While doing so, he cannot take into consideration any irrelevant fact. He cannot refuse to consider the relevant facts. He cannot shift the burden of proof. He cannot reject the relevant testimony of the witnesses only on the basis of surmises and conjectures.

Lastly, in conducting an inquiry, the rules and procedures laid down in relevant Disciplinary Action/Proceedings Regulations or Conduct Rules must be followed. In the absence of any statutory provision or specific stipulations in Conduct Regulations in this regard, the 'principles of natural justice' will be the guiding factor.

# CHAPTER 4

# INITIATION OF DISCIPLINARY ACTION/PROCEEDINGS

1. **Preliminary Investigation**
2. **Charge-sheet: (a) Drafting of Charge-sheet, (b) Change Amendment in Charge-sheet, (c) Service of Charge-sheet**
3. **Effect of Delay**
4. **Notice of Date of Hearing in Enquiry (Ex-parte Inquiry)**
5. **About Preliminary Hearing**

## 1. PRELIMINARY INVESTIGATION

Whenever management receives information/complaint or otherwise come to know that certain irregularities are going on in certain office/branch, the first step is to investigate the complaint/allegations. Preliminary Investigation usually is held to determine whether a *prima facie* case for a Disciplinary Action/Proceedings is made out. For the purpose, any officer of the Bank can be deputed.

It is very necessary for an authority to be satisfied that there are *prima facie* grounds for holding a Disciplinary Action/Proceedings and therefore he makes up his mind; he will either himself investigate or direct his subordinate to investigate the matter and it is only after he gets the result of preliminary investigations that he can decide as to whether Disciplinary Action/Proceedings is called for or not.

The main job of Investigation Officer will be—

- Firstly, to collect evidence of irregularities which he has noticed.
- Secondly, to pinpoint the culprits who in his opinion are responsible or who may be guilty of misconduct.
- Thirdly, to suggest management as to further course of action in the matter.

In view of the above, the Investigation Officer should be advised that in his investigation, there should not be gaps and all possible links leading to the misconduct and the Delinquent Officer should be made clear so that the Departmental Authority may take a pragmatic decision in relation to Disciplinary Action/Proceedings.

After completing the preliminary investigations, the department examines the report and scrutinizes the evidence available for the management and sees the recommendations of Investigation Officer and then takes a decision as to further course of action in the matter.

*There is no requirement of law that in a preliminary investigation the presence of the Delinquent Officer is required or he should be given an opportunity to participate.*

Since the preliminary Investigation Report is a kind of private document for the department and further Investigation Officer puts his personal opinions and views and moreover full report may not be useful or part may be redundant. The investigation report can be called as interdepartmental communication for facilitating management in its working. Generally, it is claimed as a privileged document. Investigation Officer is not produced as witness because his main job is to assist the department in reaching to a decision for further course of action only. Therefore, a Preliminary Investigation Report would not by itself be enough to state that a Disciplinary Action/Proceedings has been initiated.

But, when an Investigation Officer is produced as witness during inquiry and states details of investigation conducted by him, it will be necessary to produce investigation report in inquiry so that Delinquent Officer may cross-examine on the point. Here, the situation will be akin to the evidence of an investigation in a criminal trial.[1]

Ordinarily, a Delinquent Officer is not entitled to have a copy of Investigation Report unless the Inquiring Authority relies upon such report in inquiry.

## Practical Guidance

Being a fact-finding work, the Investigation Officer should be made clear in his appointment letter that he has to cover the following necessarily—

- The allegations should be investigated thoroughly.
- Whether allegations are *prima facie* appears to be substantiated or not, should be mentioned in report.

1. P. Jayachandra Rao Vs State Bank of Haryana and Others 1991(1) Bank CLR 363

- The event/transaction/*modus operandi* leading to the necessity of investigation.
- The management's evidence leading to the proof of the allegation covering oral and documentary both. Oral statement of all connected persons whether employee or independent should be taken apart from listing them as witness.
- The Delinquent Officer's version in the matter and discussions on the veracity of the Delinquent Officer's defense.
- Recommendations on each allegation giving a conclusion as to whether substantiated by the evidence.
- The preliminary investigation report should be submitted alongwith the available proofs such as statements, documents, certified copies, zerox copies etc. and he should also ensure that all sensitive documents which may be required at the time of inquiry are placed in proper custody of the concerned office preferably under dual control as per Bank's norms.

On receipt of the Investigation Report, concerned controlling office (R.O./Z.O./ H.O./L.H.O./D.O./ C.O. etc.) should send the report to the higher authorities and to the Vigilance Department (only in cases having vigilance angle) alongwith their specific comments on the malafides and motives noticed on the part of the Delinquent Officer and their specific recommendations for the proposed action. Even in cases where Vigilance department has carried out investigation, the concerned department and the controlling authority is only authorised to make recommendations on such investigation reports. Meanwhile, awaiting instructions from higher-ups draft charge-sheet should be prepared and must be kept on the record of the department.

## 2. CHARGE-SHEET

It is necessary for the management to prescribe what would be the misconduct so that the Delinquent Officer knows the pitfall he should guard against. Misconducts are already elaborated in Conduct Regulations. Still management cannot have unbridled discretion to dub any conduct as misconduct. Therefore, an officer must have an adequate advance notice of what action or what conduct would constitute misconduct. Charge in Disciplinary Action/Proceedings cannot be equated or compared with the charge as defined in Criminal Procedure Code. The concept of charge under Criminal Procedure Code is quite distinct.

Charge-sheet is a document containing charges prepared by Disciplinary Authority for and in the name of the officer employee against whom he has decided to initiate Disciplinary Action/Proceedings in case reply to same is not found satisfactory. Charge-sheet in Disciplinary Action/Proceedings is a written and formal intimation containing the alleged acts of misconducts which Delinquent Officer has committed. There is no prescribed form but full and true disclosure of the facts is must.

It also demands his explanation to the charges within a specified period and thus it is a starting point of commencement of the Disciplinary Action/Proceedings. The Disciplinary Action/Proceedings shall be deemed to have commenced only with the issuance of a charge-sheet. In terms of Conduct Regulations, drawing up of a Charge-sheet by Disciplinary Authority is the first step for initiation of a Disciplinary Action/ Proceedings. Unless and until a Charge-sheet is drawn up, a Disciplinary Action/ Proceedings for the purpose of Conduct Regulation cannot be initiated.

It is not necessary that initial *Memo* should be issued before serving the charge-sheet. The management may, if it deems fit, skip over the formality of issuing initial memo. In certain cases where the facts and circumstances are very clear and the management has no doubt about the same, it may directly issue the charge-sheet. But still it is advisable for the management to issue a memo. There may be many reasons for this, e.g., Disciplinary Authority may be far away and generally does not have first hand information, the view of employee helps management in arriving at a proper decision at the very first stage. *Memo, being an administrative action, is a matter of routine and does not bring the employee at the level of charge-sheeted employee.*

The issue of charge-sheet indicates that management has come to the conclusion that there is a *prima facie* case and therefore wants to proceed against the erring employee. The issuance of charge-sheet is the statutory compliance of one of the fundamental rules of principles of natural justice, viz., *audi alteram pertem*, i.e., "hear the other side" or no one should be condemned unheard. In case disciplinary authority takes into account allegations brought on record in the course of the proceedings but not within the ambit of the charge-sheet and gives finding thereupon, then any punishment awarded can be successfully assailed unless Conduct Regulations otherwise provide.

As far as authority to issue charge-sheet to an officer employee in the nationalised banks is concerned, it has been prescribed under respective Disciplinary Action regulations of the concerned Bank.

## (a) Drafting of Charge-sheet

The uppermost requirement in a Disciplinary Action/Proceedings is to see that charges are for misconduct or for lapses on the part of the Delinquent Officer in the course of the employment. The Rules and Regulations particularly in a public sector bank are to be strictly interpreted and where misconduct and lapses are not specifically spelt out, it should be examined whether the charges are for contravention of any Conduct Regulation or standing instructions in a manual or for any good and sufficient reason, especially the practices which are adopted over a period of years even though they may not have been accepted as a rule should be carefully analysed to see whether such practices are prevalent in the Banking industry and normally assumed the place of customary rules. An in-expert drafter makes elaborate charges by repeating the same type of misconduct in different phraseology, commonly considered as misjoinder of charges. Many times, transaction is split into parts to make an artificial distinction such as between disobedience and insubordination, indecent and righteous behaviour, misappropriation and misuse of funds. Another usual defect in drafting of charges is to lump together all acts of omissions and commissions which would not be misconduct or lapses by bringing them within mischief of general clauses of Conduct Regulation, viz., acts unbecoming of an officer or failure to take all possible steps to ensure and protect the Bank's interest or not discharging his duties with utmost honesty/devotion and diligence, or not acting in the performance of his duties and exercise of powers conferred upon him otherwise than in his best judgment. If a misconduct or lapse is covered under a specific clause of the Conduct Regulation, then it is wrong to include it in a general clause with a view to make it appear more serious. The penalties prescribed under Conduct Regulations can also be inflicted for any other good sufficient reasons which would prejudice the interest of Bank. Hence, Disciplinary Authority has been given a broad spectrum from which to draw a charge-sheet. Disciplinary Authority has to properly apply his mind before major penalty charges are leveled particularly where *prima facie* the Delinquent Officer has not committed misappropriation/fraud or indulged in any malafide or corrupt activity. Facts and only facts will be the contents leaving the inferences, judgments, conclusions. A charge-sheet need not to mention evidence whether documentary or oral. Charge-sheet must contain a plain statement of the act or omission complained against.

If the charge is incapable of being understood or not defined with sufficient certainty, it will be vague. Similarly, a charge-sheet should not assume the guilt of Delinquent Officer.

Basically, charge-sheet is a narration of facts. However, following points should be remembered while drafting charge-sheet:

(i) Charge-sheet is to be prepared and issued in accordance with the Conduct Rules and on the basis of various circulars issued by the management from time to time.

(ii) All specific cases should be incorporated in the charge-sheet.

(iii) If there is malafide aspect, it should be clearly spelt out in the Articles of charges and imputations in respect of each case.

(iv) In case procedural lapses found on other accounts are also to be included in the charge-sheet alongwith the specific cases investigated, to avoid production of large number of exhibits and the delay in witness stage, as far as possible, the accounts may be segregated under groups covering uniform lapses and the same may be given in the form of Annexure to charge-sheet. For example, in mass loans, the lapses mainly noticed are non-carrying out pre-/post-inspections, the payments were made direct to the borrowers and not to the suppliers etc. In such cases, it may be agreed that the ledger sheets/vouchers of the respective loan/savings or current deposits accounts and the oral deposition of the witnesses to the effect that no inspections were carried out, would suffice to prove the charges.

(v) At this stage, the department should also decide whether there is a requirement of opinion of handwriting expert on any disputed document and then the same should be sent to the Government handwriting expert at this stage only.

The charge-sheet should convey to the Delinquent Officer employee the exact nature of the allegation in such a way that he should understand the charge in clear terms that could enable him to meet the alleged charge. It is easier to make allegations, but not so to substantiate the same. Only charge for which adequate documentary proof is available should be incorporated in the charge-sheet. The charge should not relate to an issue which has already been the subject-matter of any earlier enquiry and decision. Even the charges/facts in issue decided in criminal case/under other proceedings should be avoided in being incorporated in charge-sheet.

Normally, the charge-sheet consists of following—

(i) **Articles of charges:** It contains in clear terms, the actual charges or allegations against the officer employee concerned.

(ii) **Statement of imputation of misconduct:** It contains details of the incident on which the charges are based. It covers ground by giving details and specific instances of the factual nature of charges.

(iii) **List of documents in support of charges:** The documents containing evidences in support of the allegations which are supposed to be listed for producing during the enquiry should be carefully scrutinised.

(iv) **List of witnesses proposed to be examined in support of charges:** A number of witnesses are usually examined during the course of the Preliminary Investigation in order to ascertain the facts of the case. The list of such witnesses should be carefully checked and only those witnesses who will be able to give positive evidence to be produced in the oral enquiry.

The charge-sheet should compulsorily afford an opportunity to the Delinquent Officer to defend himself and give proper explanation by calling written statement of defense within reasonable stipulated time. If the Delinquent Officer employee asks for extension of time for submission of reply, a reasonable extension can be granted, if the request is found to have been made on genuine grounds. However, it is clarified that charge-sheet need not contain the details of documents or the names of witnesses proposed to be examined to prove the charge or a list to that fact unless there is specific provision to that effect. Charge-sheet, in other words, is not expected to be a record of evidence. Fair procedure does not mean giving of copies of the documents or list of witnesses alongwith the charge-sheet. Of course, statement of allegation has to accompany the charge-sheet when required by Conduct Regulations.

## (b) Change/Amendment in Charge-sheet

The Disciplinary Authority can amend the charge-sheet. Generally, bank's conduct or D/A regulations are silent with regard to amendments to the charge-sheet. At the same time, there is no statutory rule or binding precedent that the Competent Authority is precluded from issuing any new charge-sheet. There may be a situation where substantial amendment to the charge-sheet might become necessary. If after serving the charge-sheet it is found that there is mistake in date, time and other facts, the management can amend the charge-sheet by way of corrigendum/addendum or the charge-sheet can be cancelled and another charge-sheet can be issued before initiation of the enquiry. Under Disciplinary Action/Proceedings, there is no bar in giving a supplementary charge-sheet if the circumstances require so[1] though there may not be any provision in this regard in Conduct Regulations.

### (c) Service of Charge-sheet

Service of charge-sheet is a necessary ingredient for initiation of Disciplinary Action/Proceedings.

The disciplinary authority should ensure that the charge-sheet is duly served to the Delinquent Officer. In case the charged employee is not available for personal service of the charge-sheet upon him, the charge-sheet should be sent to him by registered post with acknowledgement due at his last given address on the official record of the Bank or his last known address. In case the registered envelope is received back undelivered, it should be preserved unopened. However, the returned undelivered envelope with the remarks other than "refused" cannot be presumed as due service. The other alternative is to display the charge-sheet on the official noticeboard at the workplace of the charged officer.

## 3. EFFECT OF DELAY

It is necessary that the charge-sheet is served on the Delinquent Officer as early as possible, but it should not be a hasty action. When an employee secures job in Bank on wrong caste certificate of schedule tribe and after show cause, the matter is closed by Bank with a warning and after 21 years the employee is again served with a charge-sheet and domestic enquiry is conducted, the case will be of inordinate delay and it will be unfair to permit domestic enquiry to be proceeded with on[2] such charge-sheet.

Inordinate delay in initiating Disciplinary Action or in issuing Charge-sheet may amount to make the whole affair unfair. A charge-sheet should not be framed on stale material.

Where show cause notice was issued on 04/04/1981 and reply was submitted on 22/04/1981 and the same was not found satisfactory but charge-sheet was issued on 09/02/1989, the charge-sheet was quashed on the ground of delay.[3]

But delay of only four years in serving the charge-sheet to the employee cannot be in itself a ground for quashing the same and mere delay in serving charge-sheet cannot make out a case of malafides. Such technical levers may be when coupled with some substantial grounds; it can make out a defense case. But such irregularity by itself is not sufficient to give any premium to the employee.[4] Delay in inquiry may lead to the wastage and destruction of valuable pieces of evidence. Delay may also cause

---

1. N.K. Shrivastava Vs Deputy General Manager, Punjab National Bank, Lucknow and Others 2005(2) Bank CLR 712 (All)
2. K.S. Chalam Vs Bank of India and Another 1998(2) Bank CLR 271
3. Subhash Chandra Basu Vs Bank of Baroda and Others 1992(2) Bank CLR 449 Calcutta 81
4. Central Bank of India Vs T.C. Taparia 1998(1) Bank CLR 290

or compel the persons closely related to a particular incident to forget and to become unable to make the appropriate but suitable replies to the questions put to them in witness box.

While initiating Disciplinary Action/Proceeding in case of inordinate delay, management should have some reasonable explanation with it. No doubt, there may be more than one reason for delay in serving charge-sheet like irregularities did not came to light, investigation was delayed or some Court case was in existence and others as well. But one should be satisfied after all that the delay is reasonable and beyond the control of management.

## 4. NOTICE OF DATE OF HEARING IN ENQUIRY (EX-PARTE INQUIRY)

A proper notice of Inquiry should be issued to the Delinquent Officer. The practice in this regard varies in the banking industry. Some management announces the date of commencement of inquiry to the Delinquent Officer while others leave it to the Inquiring Authority. However, one should get adequate time. For subsequent sittings, no separate notice is necessary if the date, time and venue is recorded in the body of the Inquiry Proceedings and the same is noted by all concerned.

Inquiring Authority has to communicate every date to the Delinquent Officer and the Presenting Officer. Such communication of date must include venue and time also. In case of Preliminary Investigation/first date of Inquiry, the information will be sent by post and by telephone also. While other dates will be treated to have been communicated when parties take copy of the Inquiry Proceedings on the date.

Where Delinquent Officer took the plea that he received the notice of inquiry alongwith charge-sheet on the date fixed itself for hearing and therefore he informed Inquiring Authority by registered post but orders passed afterwards were never communicated and hearing was made ex-parte on several dates. Declaring the procedure adopted by Inquiring Authority in breach of principles of natural justice, it was held that when Inquiring Authority was having the changed address which was submitted at the time of previous explanation and was accepted by Inquiring Authority, the inquiry was held vitiated.[1]

In ex-parte inquiry, the evidence should be recorded that the Delinquent Officer was asked to appear before the Inquiring Authority with due acknowledgement but the Delinquent Officer has failed to report deliberately and letter/notices calling the Delinquent Officer should also be recorded in the Proceedings. In addition, copy of the Proceedings should also be sent to him under registered post so that further opportunity may be provided to him for doing the needful. In an ex-parte inquiry if the charges are borne out from the documents, kept in normal course of business of Bank, no oral evidence is necessary to prove the charge. When a Delinquent Officer chooses not to attend Disciplinary Action/Proceedings, then such Delinquent Officer

---

1. Akhileshwar Singh Vs Bihar State Co-operative Land Development Bank and Others 1992(2) Bank CLR 496 (Patna)

cannot contend that Inquiring Authority should not have relied upon the documents which were not made available or disclose to him. Of course, even in ex-parte inquiry, some evidence is necessary to establish the charges, especially when Delinquent Officer denies the charges. Uncontroverted documentary evidence is sufficient to prove the charge.[1] Thus, a Delinquent Officer, who has refused to avail the opportunities provided to him in a Disciplinary Action/Proceeding for defending himself, cannot be permitted to complain at a later stage that he has been denied a reasonable opportunity to defend himself against the charges leveled.

### Venue

The venue of the Inquiry Proceedings normally will be the place where the Delinquent Officer is serving. It can be fixed elsewhere provided there are valid and convincing reasons for the same. In any case, the interest of the Delinquent Officer is not adversely affected. The deciding factor in such cases will be the balance of convenience.

## 5. ABOUT PRELIMINARY HEARING

On the day of Preliminary hearing, Inquiring Authority should verify from the Presenting Officer of having received his appointment letter and from the Delinquent Officer about the receipt of charge-sheet and whether he admits the charge. In case the Delinquent Officer admits any or all the charges, the same has to be recorded and then a decision can be taken as to how the inquiry will be conducted and on which charges. This includes a decision on the admission whether they are sufficient to dispense with the inquiry or not.

It is also the duty of Inquiring Authority to inquire from the Delinquent Officer whether he has decided to avail the services of an Assisting Officer as provided under rules. If the Delinquent Officer decides to avail the services of an Assisting Officer, a letter should be obtained from him and declaration should be obtained from Assisting Officer that he is not appearing in more than two cases at that point of time.

On receipt of charge-sheet and appointment letters, the date will be fixed for hearing, wherein Inquiring Authority will ensure that all documents by which and a penal of witnesses by whom the articles of charges are proposed to be proved are recorded giving in description of the documents and number. During Preliminary hearing, Inquiring Authority will also direct suitably the Presenting Officer for arranging and making it convenient for inspection of the original documents listed in the charge-sheet.

While fixing next date after completion of Preliminary hearing, Inquiring Authority shall also record by an order that the Delinquent Officer may for the purpose of preparing defense:

1. State Bank of India & Others Vs Narendra Kumar Pandey AIR 2013 SC (Civil) 762

(i) Complete inspection of the documents listed in the charge-sheet furnished to him/her, immediately and in any case not later than 5 days from the date of such order if he/she had not done so earlier.

(ii) Submit a list of documents and witnesses that he/she wants for the inquiry.

(iii) Give notice within ten days of the order or within such extended time as the Inquiring Authority may allow for discovery or production of the documents referred to in (ii).

# CHAPTER 5

# PRESENTING OFFICER



## 1. PRESENTING OFFFICER

Generally, the Conduct Regulations provide for appointment of presenting officer. Disciplinary Authority, by order, may appoint a public servant to be known as Presenting Officer to present on its behalf the case in support of Articles of charge. But Inquiring Authority/Officer also has power to conduct inquiry and may question to witnesses in its own separate authority. Despite presence of relevant regulation, there is no legal compulsion that the Presenting Officer should be appointed and the mere fact that Presenting Officer was not appointed will not vitiate the inquiry. [1]

However, nationalised banks' Service Regulations make clear about the appointment of a person as Presenting Officer other than the Inquiring Authority. The burden of establishing the charge against Delinquent Officer rests on Presenting Officer. Presenting Officer works as an agent/attorney of the Competent Authority.

The Presenting Officer is a nominee of the Disciplinary Authority for presenting the management case in front of Inquiring Authority. Such presentation of case is in support of the charges leveled in the charge-sheet which has been issued to the Delinquent Officer. The general guidelines for a Presenting Officer are being below.

- Presenting Officer should be issued an appointment letter authorising him to present the case through the inquiry.

1. Prakash Vs Board of Directors, Mithila Kshetriya Gramin Bank, Darbhanga and Others 1996(1) Bank CLR 157

- Presenting Officer should acquaint himself with the details of charge, documents, witnesses as mentioned in the charge-sheet and on which/ whom management is going to rely to prove each of the charges.
- Presenting Officer must decide on the appropriate strategy for presenting in the case in an orderly manner.
- Presenting Officer is expected to manage from the concerned offices copies of documents/statement of witnesses at the time of preliminary hearing.
- Presenting Officer should also arrange for inspection of the originals as demanded by the Delinquent Officer. It is essential that Presenting Officer while making available the original records for inspection should take all possible steps to see that the documents, files etc. are not tampered with or destroyed. He should be present throughout when the inspection is in progress, he should not delegate someone to deputise him when the inspection of the documents is in progress.
- He should not give all the files, papers at one time, but should handover file by file and document by document for inspection. All the papers in the file should be serially numbered. A note to the effect that the file containing papers bearing serial number 1 to be made in the file. The Delinquent Officer may be permitted to take notes from the documents.
- Presenting Officer often examines the witnesses only to support the documentary evidence listed and recorded during the Preliminary hearing as majority of the documentary evidence are Bank's own documents. There is no need to discuss each document and get them supported through examination of management witnesses for this process alone. Quite a number of sittings are wasted instead, while recording the documentary evidences. It should be ensured to record the description of each document. Of course, in respect of certain documents, if the Presenting Officer feels that these should be discussed through examination of management witness for bringing out certain inherent or inferring factors, the same should be done. Likewise if independent documents/statements are filed as exhibits, the same should also be supported by the writer or signatory, if it is found necessary.
- Presenting Officer should also assist the Inquiring Authority in arranging for making available additional documents as required by the defense/ Delinquent Officer.
- Presenting Officer has to put forth his argument before the Inquiring Authority in regard to the demand of the Delinquent Officer for the documents which management does not understand fit for inspection of the Delinquent Officer so that the Inquiring Authority may give its ruling on the point.
- Cross-examination of a management witness should be attended by the Presenting Officer with attention and alertness in order to note the

contradictions which have crept in either with examination-in-chief or previous answers given in cross-examination. Any such contradictions and any incomplete subject left, the same may be clarified during the re-examination of the witness. Further, the management witness should not be made a subject by the assisting officer to scandalous, indecent, irrelevant and annoying questions.

- Availability of management witness has to be ensured by Presenting Officer in advance so that the next date may be obtained from Inquiring Authority accordingly. Presenting Officer should take steps to ensure that witness is informed of the date and remains present on the fixed date.
- Whenever a management witness appears to have made such answers which are either incorrect or there is deviation from the previous statement of the same witness or otherwise in overall view, the witness appears to have been on the side of the Delinquent Officer, the Presenting Officer should not hesitate in declaring such witness 'as hostile' and then he will have a right to ask leading questions to the witness and simultaneously the credibility of the witness will be shaken.
- Overenthusiasm, extra involvement in proving the charges may take a somersault and therefore the Presenting Officer will be well advised not to fabricate, prepare the evidence/documents. Presenting Officer should always understand that he is a part of the big system where every tool has to perform its assigned work and not more than that.
- Presence of Presenting Officer during the inquiry thoroughly is the requirement of his job and in no case inquiry should be adjourned due to his absence leaving the circumstances beyond control. On the other hand, the endeavour of the Presenting Officer should be to highlight the frivolousness of the adjournments which are being taken by the Assisting Officer unnecessarily.
- Written briefs should be submitted within the stipulated period as directed by Inquiring Authority. Written briefs should contain detailing on each charge and relevancy of the evidence how the same proves the charge.

Further, at the time of presentation of the management's case, Presenting Officer should put forth the charge and present the documents relied upon to prove the charges before the Inquiring Authority in a systematic manner. In examination of the witnesses, Presenting Officer should during the examination-in-chief ensure that only relevant questions are asked. Here, relevancy means that only such questions should be asked in examination-in-chief which leads to the proving of the charge. He should avoid from asking leading questions. Leading questions cannot be allowed to be asked to management witnesses by forcing them to say only 'yes'.[1] Practically,

---

1. Braj Bhushan Shukla Vs G.M. (Operation- I ), Appellate Authority, UCO Bank & Another 2012 (2) DRT Cases 484 (Allahabad High Court)

a Presenting Officer has to plan the questions intended to be asked to be precise and in a manner which makes the witness give a detailed answer as required for proving the charges. Frivolous/irrelevant questions should not be asked. It is noticeable that an Assisting Officer can ask leading questions in the cross-examination and Presenting Officer will not be having any opportunity to object such questions.

In sum and substance, the major role envisaged for the Presenting Officer in support of the charges has to be performed by assisting the Inquiring Authority and in ensuring that the Inquiry Proceedings are conducted in a fair and just manner without any unwarranted and uncalled for delay.

# CHAPTER 6

# EVIDENCE UNDER INQUIRY

**1. Supply of Documents**

**2. Witness: (a) Cross-examination, (b) Re-examination**

Preponderance of probability is the only guiding principle for standard of proof in a Disciplinary Action/Proceedings. But this preponderance of probability will not only be applicable in case of bringing charges at home but in case of defense as well.

Strict rules of evidence are not applicable to Disciplinary Action/Proceedings. So far as proof is concerned, the law is that, in some cases, proof may be only documentary and in some cases, oral. The requirement of proof depends on the facts and circumstances of each case.[1] The only requirement of law is that the allegations against the Delinquent Officer must be established by such evidence acting upon which a reasonable person acting reasonably and with objectivity may arrive at a finding upholding the gravity of charge. Mere conjecture and surmises cannot sustain the findings of guilt in Disciplinary Action/Proceedings.

The sophisticated rules of Court evidence are not applicable under inquiry. All materials which are logically probative for a prudent mind are permissible. There is no allergy to hearsay evidence provided it has reasonable nexus and credibility to the facts of the case. Similarly, discrepancies in evidence may occur due to time lag between the complaint and the date of inquiry.

Law is well settled that Court will not interfere with the findings of the Inquiring Authority unless it is satisfied that the evidence collected during the inquiry is such

1. State Bank of India & Others Vs Narendra Kumar Pandey AIR 2013 SC (Civil) 762

that no reasonable person can come to the conclusion that the Delinquent Officer is guilty of the charge. Unless it is established that there is no material on record to support the charge, the Courts ordinarily decline to interfere.[1] Inadequacy or insufficiency of evidence is not a matter for consideration for the Courts while reviewing inquiry provided there is some evidence to support the conclusions of inquiry report.

## 1. SUPPLY OF DOCUMENTS

Under inquiry, it is not necessary that each and every document must be supplied to the Delinquent Officer but only material and relevant documents are necessary to be supplied. If a document though mentioned in charge-sheet is not relevant to the charges leveled or if not referred or relied upon by Inquiring Authority in holding the charges as proved, no exception can be taken to the legality of proceedings.

Supreme Court[2] has held that non-supply of documents on which the Inquiring Authority does not rely during the course of inquiry does not create any prejudice to the Delinquent Officer.

It is only those documents which are relied upon by the Inquiring Authority to arrive at his conclusion the non-supply of which would cause prejudice being violative of 'principle of natural justice'. Even then, the non-supply of those documents prejudice the case of the Delinquent Officer has to be established. Where Delinquent Officer asked for copies of all those bills which were submitted by himself before the authority, Supreme Court[3] held that there is no prejudice whatsoever and accordingly dismissal order was upheld.

However, where charge-sheet contains list of documents which are proposed to be utilised, but copies of such listed documents are not supplied to the Delinquent Officer in spite of his request and at the same time he is called upon to submit his reply an effective opportunity to defend cannot be inferred.

Mere non-production of register and ledger even after specific demand from the side of employee where employee has been allowed access to original vouchers which were in his own handwriting forming basis of Disciplinary Action/Proceedings, will not be of much importance because the same has not caused any prejudice to the case of employee.[4]

Similarly, where the Delinquent Officer does not take objection before Inquiring Authority regarding non-supplying of documents relied upon by management of the Bank, the same cannot be taken at writ Court for the first time.[5] Where sub-manager

---

1. Ishwar Chandra Mahanta Vs Orrissa State Co-operative Agriculture and Rural Development Bank Ltd. 2002(1) Bank CLR 74 (ORI)
2. Syndicate Bank and Others Vs Venkatesh Gururao Kurati 2006(1) Bank CLR 430 (S.C.)
3. Bank of India Vs T. Jogram 2008(1) Bank CLR 161 (S.C.)
4. Padam Chand Jain Vs Chairman, Central Bank of India 1991(1) Bank CLR 112
5. Dwarika Roy Vs Allahabad Bank and Others 1995(1) Bank CLR 192

took the plea that he worked on oral instructions of Branch Manager in issuing four delivery orders of 34 aluminum coils in favour of constituent without receiving corresponding payment for such delivery and Branch Manager was cited as witness but was not produced on inquiry floor, and a witness not having personal knowledge was produced, it was held that findings under inquiry were arrived at without in such a manner that no reasonable prudent man on given material could have reached such a conclusion and accordingly the inquiry was quashed.[1]

Similarly, where Inquiring Authority allows any document after the defense case is completed without providing any opportunity to the Delinquent Officer to rebut it, such evidence will make the inquiry bad. Because if such document could have been produced during the inquiry, the Delinquent Officer could have cross-examined upon such documents. Even if the documents are signed by the Delinquent Officer, the position will remain the same.

Where documents are in power and possession of the management, Supreme Court[2] laid down *"At inquiry if the Delinquent Officer seeks to support his defense with reference to any of the documents in the custody of the management or the department, then the documents either may be summoned or copies thereof may be given at the request and cost of the Delinquent officer."* Thus, where charges for distributing fictitious loans and during inquiry, the Delinquent Officer asks for statement of account, the same will be very much relevant as the Delinquent Officer can show that the loans are being operated and moneys are being deposited and loan accounts are not fictitious. An Inquiring Authority is not permitted to collect any material from outside sources during the conduction of inquiry.

If Bank Officials are of the view that any particular document is confidential in nature and a copy thereof cannot be handed over to the Delinquent Officer, they may so indicate in writing to the employee and it will be open to the Inquiring Authority to examine whether the denial of such copy would amount to violation of 'principles of natural justice.'[3]

In another matter when Bank refused the documents to the Delinquent Officer because they were not relevant in the opinion of the Bank, it was held whether the documents are relevant or not has to be judged from the point view of defense of the Delinquent Officer and since the charges were based on documents the stand of Bank in denying access to those documents does have a deleterious and damaging effect on defense.[4]

---

1. Venkatarama Murlidhar Shenoy Vs Syndicate Bank 2001(2) Bank CLR 48 (Calcutta)
2. Management Kisan Degree College Vs Shambhu Saran Pandey and Others 1995(70) FLR 352 (S.C.)
3. Prathama Bank, Head Office Moradabad, through its Chairman Vs Vijay Kumar Goel, 1990(1) Bank CLR (S.C.) AIR 1989 S.C. 1977
4. Prakash Vs Board of Directors, Mithila Kshetriya Gramin Bank, Darbhanga 1996(1) Bank CLR 157 (Patna)

## 2. WITNESS

To be a witness means imparting knowledge in respect of relevant facts by means of oral statement or statement in writing by a person who has personal knowledge of the facts to be communicated to a Court or to a person holding inquiry or investigation. A person is said to be a witness to a certain state of facts which has to be determined by a Court or by an authority authorised to come to a decision by testifying what he has seen or something he has heard or giving his opinion in respect of controversy as an expert.

It is always open to the management to examine such witness as it chooses in Disciplinary Action/Proceedings and if it does not examine any witness it takes the risk of case being held as not proved and the mere fact that it does not examine any witness cannot vitiate inquiry.

Hence, non-availability of witness for the management does not cause any prejudice to the Delinquent Officer and in some cases management may not be in a position to prove the case due to non-availability of witness.

Thus, it is always open to the Bank either to examine or not to examine a particular witness and in case the Delinquent Officer wants any person to be examined as a witness it is up to the Delinquent Officer to produce such witness at inquiry floor.[1]

The proper rule or order of witnesses is that the management should lead the evidence first. Having charge-sheeted the Delinquent Officer, it is natural to call upon the management to produce its witnesses first. There may be situations when the witnesses in chronological order are not available for examination but it will not make any difference and available witnesses may be examined/cross-examined immediately pending the examination of unattending witnesses. If an employee avoids/refuses to participate in Disciplinary Action/Proceedings, it cannot be complained that opportunity of hearing has not been provided. Where the Delinquent Officer was supplied with a copy of report of Inquiring Authority but he did not submit any reply and notices were published, the ex-parte inquiry was upheld.[2]

Normally, the evidence on which the charges are sought to be proved must be led at the inquiry in the presence of Delinquent Officer himself. Recording of evidence in presence of Delinquent Officer serves an important purpose the witness knows that he is giving evidence against a particular person who is present before him and therefore he is cautious in making his statement. Besides there is no room for persuading the witness to make convenient statement and lastly it is easier for Delinquent Officer to cross-examine such witness whose statement has been recorded in his presence.

---

1. Shyam Nandan Prasad Singh Vs Punjab National Bank and Others 1998(2) Bank CLR 43 (Patna)
2. Chairman, Ganga Yamuna Gramin Bank and Others Vs Devi Sahai 2009(1) Bank CLR 490 (S.C.)

The idea of recording statement behind the back of Delinquent Officer, i.e., ex-parte statement and then producing the witness for cross-examination with previously recorded statement will not be the normal procedure of inquiry. Unless there are some compelling reasons before Inquiring Authority to do so, the normal procedure should be followed and all evidence should be recorded in the presence of Delinquent Officer who stands charged with the commission of acts constituting misconduct. Where application of Delinquent Officer for recording examination-in-chief in his presence afresh was turned down by Inquiring Authority and Disciplinary Authority and the Delinquent Officer cross-examined the witness on basis of examination-in-chief recorded in his absence, the inquiry was held vitiated.[1]

A statement taken behind the back of the person charged is not to be as substantive evidence and that such statement can form part of the substantive evidence only when the persons who make statement are examined before the Domestic Tribunal and the facts referred to in the statement are spoken to or affirmed before Inquiring Authority. It is true, it is not necessary for the person who has given the statements behind the back of the person charged to speak word by word or sentence by sentence before the Tribunal but the facts referred to in the statement should be affirmed at least in a general way in his evidence.

Normally, the evidence on which the charges are sought to be proved must be laid in the enquiry itself in the presence of the Delinquent Officer and unless there are compelling reasons the Inquiring Authority should not bring on record the previously recorded statement of the witnesses or to record statements of witnesses before itself ex-parte and then produce the witnesses before the Delinquent Officer concerned for cross-examination after furnishing him a copy of those previously recorded statements. Where in a case, the Inquiring Authority in his report as well as the Disciplinary Authority had formed the opinion that the misconduct was established against the petitioner on the basis of collective consideration of the evidence of those witnesses who had their previously recorded statements accepted to be their correct statements as well as the evidence of those witnesses to whom their previously recorded statements were neither read out nor they themselves read the same yet accepted the same as their statements. That being so, the Inquiring Authority was not justified in bringing on record the previously recorded statements even of those witnesses who had neither themselves read the statements nor the same were read out to them by Inquiring Authority or by the Presenting Officer.

The Disciplinary Authority also should not have relied on such statements while passing the impugned order of termination of petitioner's service. Thus, the Inquiring Authority violated the well settled principles of natural justice which vitiated the whole proceedings and consequently the order of the petitioner's dismissal was bad and could not be sustainable in law.[2] Thus, in a case Disciplinary Authority passed its order stating—

1. Vyasa Bank Ltd. Vs M. Namadev Pal and Another 1994(1) Bank CLR 405
2. Raj Kishore Pandey Vs Rewa Sidhi Gramin Bank and Others 1989(2) Bank CLR 310

*"The Presenting Officer has submitted 28 exhibits most of which are in the form of certificates of Shri Rajinder Paul and B.B. Bhatia Officer and the then assistant manager of the branch, while one document (PEX- 26) is in the form of inspection/investigation report of Shri V.B. Jindal and Shri J.R. Sharma. The certificates of inspection-cum-investigation reports are most comprehensive documents.*

*........ All the four officers appeared before the Inquiring Authority and testify to their authorship of the documents. Their certificates/inspection-cum-investigation report comprehensively cover all the allegations/charges made/leveled in the charge-sheet. They have also been supported by the documents..."*

However, during inquiry, no opportunity was given for cross-examination either the makers of report Mr. V.P. Jindal and Mr. J.R. Sharma or the officers who had granted such certificates. Consequently, denial opportunity was observed and inquiry was set aside.[1] When outside witnesses submitted a joint application before Inquiring Authority declining to come forward for cross-examination but confirming their statements, the procedural error leading to manifest injustice was observed and inquiry was set aside.[2]

In another matter where outside witness/borrower statements were produced but outside witnesses did not attend inquiry, the Court taken into consideration that—

1. The substantive evidence in relation to the charge was available only with the borrowers and other persons who not being in the employment of the Bank were not under its control and the Bank was not in a position to compel their appearance in the Disciplinary Action/Proceedings.
2. The Bank made an effort to get borrowers examined as witness in the inquiry.
3. It was established from the evidence that it was the Delinquent Officer who was behind the borrowers in making them refused to come and to depose against him in the inquiry.
4. Under the circumstances, the Bank took the only possible course of action and brought before Inquiring Authority the statement of these borrowers recorded at earlier occasions.
5. Persons who had recorded the statements of the borrower and who produced the same before the Inquiring Authority had no apparent motive to falsely implicate the Delinquent Officer; held that no infirmity in Disciplinary Action/Proceedings and punishment exists.[3]

The statements under Section 161, Cr PC may not be admissible in the criminal trial, but the said statements can be produced in a Disciplinary Action/Proceedings.

---

1. S.C. Girotra Vs United Commercial Bank and Others 1996(1) Bank CLR 248 S.C.
2. Rampal Chauhan Vs Marwar Gramin Bank and Another 2005(1) Bank CLR 381 (Rajasthan)
3. Kameshwar Singh Vs Canara Bank, Karnataka and Others 1993(1) Bank CLR 460 (Patna)

The person who made the statement has been examined before the Inquiring Authority. Statement recorded under Section 161, Cr PC was read over to the witness who admitted the contents thereof. In this way, the earlier statement under Section 161 Cr PC became a part of the examination-in-chief of the witness before the Inquiring Authority. It is not in dispute that the said statement has been given to the employee in advance and full opportunity was granted to the employee to cross-examine the said witnesses. This being the case, it is difficult to appreciate as to how the High Court could have come to the conclusion that the inquiry proceedings stood vitiated.[1]

Where copies of statement were not furnished to the Delinquent Officer and he failed to take any objection at inquiry stage that such non-furnishing has disabled him to cross-examine effectively and Court found no prejudice has been caused, the inquiry was upheld and requirement of 'principles of natural justice' was fulfilled.[2]

Where for the purpose of confirming the verbal instructions given to the Delinquent Officer, the Delinquent Officer requested for production of two witnesses after the closure of management case the denial of request made by Inquiring Authority on the ground of being irrelevant was held not to vitiate inquiry.[3]

Where charges were of shouting and using of abusing language, but during inquiry, the management witness didn't support the allegations and stated that Delinquent Officer was only talking fast and in angry tone making complaint of management over deduction in salary, the finding of guilt was not supported by Court.[4]

### (a) Cross-examination

The purpose of cross-examination is defined and definite and comprises following:

(a) Eliciting, picking and highlighting contradiction.

(b) Bringing out favourable statements.

(c) Destroying the credibility of evidence by discrediting the witness.

(d) Unfolding and finding new evidence.

Now, we will discuss above purposes one by one—

The first object of cross-examination is to make the witness contradict himself or forcing the witness to take contradictory stands or conflicting positions not only in respect of his own testimony but also in respect of the testimony of other witnesses as well as also in relation to the evidence in the shape of documents, papers which

---

1. State Bank of Bikaner and Jaipur Vs Srinath Gupta and Another 1996(2) Bank CLR 288
2. State Bank of Patiala Vs S.K. Sharma 1996(II) Labour Law Judgment 296, 1996(2) Bank CLR 59 (S.C.), 1996 Bankers' Journal 447 (S.C.), Judgment Today 1996(3) (S.C.) 722
3. Debotosh Pal Choudhry Vs Punjab National Bank and Others 2003(1) Bank CLR 654 (S.C.)
4. Braj Bhushan Shukla Vs G.M. (Operation - I), Appellate Authority, UCO Bank and Another 2012(2) DRT Cases 484 (Allahabad High Court)

are on record. The object also lies in reducing the worth, gravity and rigour of the testimony by diluting the same which will result making the testimony non-damaging to the case of defense. Whenever a witness is tendered, his evidence generally is considered to be in favour of the party which has produced the witness or which has brought the witness. With this proposition in mind, the cross-examiner attempts to break the testimony of the witness and to reduce or annihilate the force of the testimony.

This is very much necessary for proper or effective defense and if this object is not in the mind of cross-examiner, the cross-examination may reach nowhere. Because it will be very natural for the witness to affirm and confirm his testimony as stands in examination-in-chief and to put a label of truth on his previous statements.

Though a witness might have made statements in examination-in-chief yet, he might be a tutored witness possessing very little knowledge or no knowledge of the relevant fact. In examination-in-chief, the statement may be like a parrot totally tutored; words are there but no knowledge. When a cross-examination is of the standard in making the witness admit that the witness did not possess any personal knowledge or that the witness has acquired such knowledge through other persons, the worth of testimony is erased substantially. Sometimes, it is quite possible to make the witness admit that he does not exactly remember the facts and that he had no recollection of ancillary facts and circumstances. The witness may even state that he does not know the relevant facts or most relevant facts and a witness may be placed in such a position of having to admit that his statement in examination-in-chief was altogether baseless or that it was totally devoid of any substance. A witness may be compelled to face the contradictory statements made by other witnesses or there might be substantial and material contradictions between the statement of a witness on one hand and facts contained in documents and papers on the other hand. If such contradictions or other material is brought on record through the effective cross-examination, the cross-examination can be said to have achieved the desirable.

The second object of bringing out the favourable reply which may colour the charges in entirely different manner. A witness might have been very assertive and empathetical in examination-in-chief and might have supported management's case in a formidable manner. But if in the course of cross-examination such witness can be compelled to admit that the understanding was erroneous or that besides the allegations as formed in the charge-sheet, there were many other factors and circumstances justifying the particular course of conduct on the part of the Delinquent Officer, then the success on defense can be attributed. The defense can sometimes succeed in making the witness admit that the actions or acts said to be done by the Delinquent Officer were not really the acts or actions of the Delinquent Officer but are of some other employee or the Delinquent Officer was working under instructions received from the superiors. Naturally, the management will never bring on record such evidence or material on the floor of inquiry.

Charge-sheet itself might have taken some matter in isolation without considering the various other and allied factors because such factors might have helped to destroy the charge itself. Further, under certain circumstances, the cross-examiner can make the witness admit that now a different interpretation could be placed on the facts or that the same subject-matter can be understood in two or more different lines or patterns. A witness can also be compelled in cross-examination that the acts attributed to the Delinquent Officer had in fact originated from some other employee and the Delinquent Officer not directly responsible for such acts. The bonafides of the Delinquent Officer and the absence of malafides can also be brought on record through cross-examination. Cross-examination of these lines altogether and the facts, such as they are, can be interpreted in favour of the Delinquent Officer against the spirit of charge-sheet. Such cross-examination will definitely help to advance the case of the Delinquent Officer and even where it is not possible to get him exonerated altogether, the conduct and acts attributed to the Delinquent Officer can now be seen in a more favourable light. This is the second object of cross-examination.

The third object of cross-examination is to discredit the witness and expose the lack of credibility of his testimony, thereby destroying the witness himself. A witness may not have any personal knowledge. Therefore, this evidence is the product of tutoring. The witness might have obtained second hand or third hand information from others and his testimony might be based on such hearsay. The witness might have marked bias and prejudice towards the Delinquent Officer and he may be personally interested and even anxious to see that the Delinquent Officer receives some punishment or other. If this position can be established, it will expose the witness as a person highly motivated, biased and prejudiced against the Delinquent Officer and his testimony will not receive the approval of the Inquiring Authority. It may also be possible to expose the witness as a person having little or no regard for truth and facts. In other words, the witness is exposed as a liar, person coming out with false and untrue statements.

It is also possible that the witness might be tendering evidence under duress or undue influence or intimidation etc. of the Disciplinary Authority or any other management official. Inducement of the witness may be the reason for his appearance in support of charge-sheet. Inducement may be of something positive in the sense that the witness is likely to receive some benefit in return for justifying falsely against for his own involvement in the matter or due to misconduct of the witness himself. Management witness can always be biased in favour of management and also against the Delinquent Officer. If the cross-examiner is able to establish any of the above, the credibility of the witness goes to air leaving the management without evidence.

The fourth, uncovering of fresh evidence lies in the fact when a cross-examiner is capable to bring any other facts which have escaped notice of the management or the Presenting Officer. Such evidence though existed all along but management was unaware of the existence of such evidence or due to negligent working of the concerned authority, the same was tried to be suppressed and if, such evidence could have been brought to the floor of the inquiry, the charges cannot be sustained or the charges loose their ground. For instance, there might be certain records, letters or entries in the ledgers, day-book, registers which if properly considered and appreciated would have the effect of destroying the very foundation of the charges. In office working, it happens many times that to avoid some blue-eyed boys, evidences are interpreted by the management only to fix the Delinquent Officer and any such effort can be highlighted during cross-examination by compelling the witness to face the reality as exists. Instances are common where management/Disciplinary Authority know certain fact but deliberately attempted to shut out such relevant facts from the record of the Inquiry Proceedings. While such evidence is relevant and material, the logical inference will be that the proceedings are only to victimise the Delinquent Officer. Thus, if the facts which the management attempted to suppress are really vital and material and serve to demolish the charges in their entirety, the inference to be drawn is more than obvious.

Lastly, on what lies a cross-examination should be made, on what matters it should be confined, how to commence it, where to conclude and when to stop will be the questions if asked will provide the entry to the technique of cross-examination. Now, we will discuss the nature of contradiction or *practical aspects of a cross-examination,* especially in reference to banking.

In case if charge-sheet is for riotous behaviour mentioning time of occurrence at 12.15 p.m. In cross-examination, the examiner hammered away at the witness and made him admit that the occurrence was at 12.40 p.m. and not at 12.15 p.m. as stated in the charge-sheet. Though undoubtedly, it is a contradiction. However, how such contradiction is going to help in establishing the case of defense? Particularly, when time is not the essence of the charge, the contradiction will be liable to be ignored as a minor discrepancy of cross-examination in time factor. Because the real question is; did any event or incident or occurrence took place as narrated in the charge-sheet? If the occurrence took place really, it will be of little importance what the time was whether 12.00 p.m., 12.15 p.m. or 12.40 p.m.

A management's witness provided a sketchy detail for the visit of Regional Manager at the events that took place during such visit. The witness might have even stated in examination-in-chief the details of dress and colour of dress of the Regional Manager and in cross-examination, the examiner is able to bring contradiction in colour and description of dress up to some extent. Such contradiction might have had some relevance that it could be related to the identity of the person involved. However, when there is no dispute as to identity of the person and the dress which was put on by the person on that particular occasion, the contradiction is not going to make any material difference to the facts of the case. Minor inconsistency or contradictions in testimony will be treated as petty and not having any bearing on the final adjudication in the matter. The cross-examiner has to concentrate on the major points and any substantial variation or inconsistency or conflict in testimony will be of helping nature in destroying the management's case. Therefore, a cross-examiner should concentrate on the material and essential contradiction and should not waste his time and energy on trivial matters which will not effect the course of the Proceedings or Inquiry Findings. But it does not mean that minor contradictions are worthless. Actually, the crux of the matter is how much such contradictions can be utilised and how they can be coloured as contradictions of substantial nature. Therefore, efforts should be to exploit a minor contradiction by tagging the same with material facts so that such facts can be made doubtful or of no value in the eyes of Inquiring Authority/Disciplinary Authority.

On what specific points, the cross-examination should revolve. It is imperative that for the purpose/ingredients of various charges and thorough analysis of the charge-sheet will be the lighting factor. The factual part of the charge can even be taken for granted because it cannot be refuted altogether but it is the charge-part, viz., the misconduct attributed can be the focal point for cross-examination and effort should be to destroy the evidence of the witness in relation to such focal point and therefore, as a necessary corollary, the cross-examination should take into account the testimony deposed in examination-in-chief in respect of each important ingredient of the charge. Here also when the witness is not sure about the facts or unable to recollect the facts properly, the course should be to refrain from cross-examining the witness on those points because it will be wastage of time. Though in cross-examination a witness may be assisted in recollecting his memory, provided such process can help to bring on record reply favourable to the Delinquent Officer. Considerable caution should be the rule in probing the witness. When a witness pretends ignorance or lack of memory on points which are favourable to the cross-examiner or defense, it is very much necessary to probe into the memory of the witness to make him come out with facts provided the defense can visualise and must be sure that such recollection will be favourable to the defense otherwise the weapon may cause enormous damage.

Where Presenting Officer has left some material facts in his examination-in-chief, there is no need to touch those sleeping facts in cross-examination. Sometimes, an intelligent Presenting Officer will lead his witness up to a particular point and then will make the witness silent. For instance, the Presenting Officer may ask the witness about the visit to a particular godown, inspection and verification of stocks, the detection of shortage of stocks and also the inferior quality of goods and materials stored in the godown, the question may be carefully framed so that the witness speaks to the visits to the godown, the inspection and verification of stocks and the fact that there was shortage and that the quality of the goods stored did not correspond to the quality as reflected in the stock statements or invoices etc. The Presenting Officer would bank on the defense probing further into the matter by putting questions on the following lines:

(i) What was the actual amount of shortage?

(ii) In respect of what materials was the shortage detected?

(iii) Where were the goods stored and what was their condition?

(iv) You said, the quality of the material stored was poor. What exactly was the quality of the material when you inspected them?

The witness then comes out with a very good, clear and emphatic answer which will nail the Delinquent Officer on the cross. The cross-examiner should therefore be alert and should not walk into such traps. But his general approach should be to question the correctness of the facts themselves, without going into too many details, unless the details themselves are helpful, for example; a part of one item of goods might have been stored in one place and another at the store in another part in the same godown. If the verification during inspection did not take into account the second part, that can be effectively brought out and the defense can then take up the position that there was no actual shortage. But if the facts are otherwise, the approach of the defense to probe further into the matter would be totally self-defeating and the defense would have only recorded what the Prosecution was itself unable to.

**Limits of the Cross-examination**

Cross-examination is not a battle of wits between the cross-examiner and the witness. The cross-examiner should not regard a cross-examination as an opportunity to establish his intellectual superiority or supremacy over the witness. It is the opportunity given to defense to bring out the contradictions in testimony, make the witness admit that other interpretations or inferences are possible or that totally different colour can be attributed to the facts or to destroy the credibility of witness and of his testimony. If the questions are logical and relevant, there is no limit for cross-examination on the basis of time or the number of questions. Actually, the limit to cross-examination is the amount of information one can get out of the witness. Therefore, when the questions reach the saturation point and nothing further or better can be asked or can be obtained from witness, the limit for cross-examination can be said to have been reached.

Another area where caution should be the rule will be when certain questions have brought out considerable material favourable to the defense. In such situation, any further questions to the witness might help the witness to clarify or explain or to give a colour to his replies which may be unfavourable to the defense. Actually, on every question, the cross-examiner should ask to himself whether he should ask the question and whether the reply will be favourable to him. If the reply goes against the defense, what will be repercussions of such reply? When one should stop in asking questions is a matter of experience on one side and nature of witness on the other side. When the witness is very empathetic and firm in his replies and does not yield any ground, it would be purposeless to continue such questioning because every further answer will cement the case management. So far as limits of area where a cross-examination should run over is concerned, the cross-examiner should have an introspection of himself and scrutiny of the material emanated from the cross-examination; whether he has been able to bring on record contradictions, glaring inconsistencies, remarkable conflicts, apparent mistakes in the testimony etc. and has he succeeded in destroying the credibility of the witness. Once credibility of the witness is wiped out, there is no need to cross-examine further on any other point.

**In respect of documentary evidence,** the exhibits marked in the Disciplinary Action/Proceedings should be approached with great care and caution. The witness under cross-examination may not have any personal or direct knowledge of the contents of the documents. Yet, he might have spoken freely about the contents in examination-in-chief. The defense can attack the witness successfully and establish that he has no personal knowledge of the contents.

The witness under cross-examination may not be competent to answer questions in relation to the contents of the documents. In such cases also, the defense should succeed in establishing that the witness is not competent to answer the question as to the contents and once that stage is successfully achieved, rest of the cross-examination on that particular point may be stopped. The defense can and should try to establish contradictions between the contents of the document and the oral testimony of the witness. If the witness is tendering evidence totally opposed to the contents of the document, the resultant position would be favourable to the defense when the document in question is a management exhibit. The management cannot take the stand about its documents and other papers that the witness has uttered falsehood or *vice versa* that the witness has spoken the truth and the document is wrong. Contradictions of this nature and magnitude destroy the credibility of both kinds of evidences, viz., documentary and oral and the same will be nullified and non-existing. The cross-examiner can put the questions to the witnesses to bring out the bias, motivation prior enmity, inducement and various other matters. However, in a Disciplinary Action/ Proceedings, the defense will not be permitted to attack or impeach the personal conduct or character of the witness. It is certainly open to attack the conduct of the witness insofar as his involvement in the transactions pertaining to the charges is concerned. A cross-examiner cannot be bound to limit its cross-examination but what the witness has testified to in examination-in-chief. The cross-examiner has a much wider latitude and it is open to him to go beyond the charges for the purpose of establishing certain relevant facts and also for attributing motive, bias or prejudice etc. to the witness.

When a management witness replies in such a way as "I don't know; I don't remember; I am not sure; I have no personal knowledge; It may be so or may not be so etc.", the cross-examination can be said diluting the force of the testimony. If the defense through cross-examination is able to make the witness take up the position repeatedly – "I can't answer this question; I am unable to answer this question; I refuse to answer this question; I will not answer this question; I don't know the answer of this question," then the examiner scored a major point. When the witness refuses to answer a question, the logical inference is that such refusal is for the specific purpose of suppressing vital material and relevant facts. It may also be that the witness refuses to answer such questions because he is afraid of to reveal his involvement in the matter and if such questions answered may put him where he incriminate himself. If such replies are given by the witness to a chain of questions and that too for many vital and important questions, the argument can be advanced that witness does not intend to come out with truth of the matter and therefore the testimony of the witness should be discarded.

A document may be partly in favour of one party and partly in favour of another partly, i.e., in case of Disciplinary Action/Proceedings partly in favour of management and partly in favour of defense. However, a party relying on a document cannot resile from the part and the documents will be treated for the purpose of inquiry as one and the effect of entire document will be considered. Therefore, when the defense produce a document which is partly against the Delinquent Officer, then defense cannot rely only on that portion which is suitable to it and discard which is not favourable to it and *vice versa.* In case of management exhibit, defense can legitimately frame questions in respect of only that part favourable to it and ignore the other part which is not favourable to it. Therefore, defense should always be cautious in introducing any document weighing the pros and cons whether the unfavourable portion of the document is substantial or outweigh the favourable portion and the document should not be brought on the record of the inquiry. In the other case if the document is overwhelmingly in favour of the defense and the negative portion is minimal, such document can be used for the purpose of cross-examination of management witness. Cross-examination is essentially leading in character and questions that are put in a cross-examination are direct questions so that the witness either affirm or deny the statements reflected in the question as to suit the defense. Questions in cross-examination should not provide an opportunity to the witness to come out with explanations or clarifications. The purpose of putting direct questions to the witness in cross-examination is to pin the witness down to certain defending positions. Suggestions can also be put to the witness and the witness can be asked either to accept or to deny the suggestion. Always the questions in cross-examination should be so framed that the witness does not have any opportunity to reaffirm the correctness of the testimony tendered by him in examination-in-chief. On the other hand, it should be the attempt of cross-examiner to bring out contradictions, inconsistencies, bias etc. on the part of the witness.

Letters or statements or complaints have to be proved at two different stages, viz., the formal proof of the document that is, in relation to its genuineness and authenticity and thereafter regarding the contents of the document. It is the basic rule that a written statement given by the witness prior to the commencement of the inquiry proceedings should not be used as evidence against the Delinquent Officer if the author or maker of the document is not produced as a witness and is not subject to cross-examination. The defense should therefore object to the marking of such documents as exhibits in the Inquiry Proceedings.

Cross-examination is a very powerful weapon in the hands of the defense. The weapon should be wielded carefully and to the advantage of the Delinquent Officer. When the cross-examiner is not able to decide on what points he should cross-examine the witness or whether the witness has given very clear and specific replies, the better and safer course would be to refrain oneself from further cross-examining rather than embarking upon a purposeless and bad cross-examination. No cross-examination is certainly better and safer than a bad cross-examination.

### (b) Re-examination

After cross-examination is completed, the Inquiring Authority may permit the management to re-examine in case of ambiguity or there is a need to clarify certain replies. However, it will not be open to the management to bring fresh evidence or additional evidence in the course of re-examination and the defense will be well within its rights to object to such questions.

The advantage to Delinquent Officer which he has procured in cross-examination cannot be allowed to be taken away through re-examination. No doubt, Inquiring Authority is rested with wide discretion but such powers should not be exercised unless there are proper circumstances in favour of such motion. To find out the truth and render just decision, re-examination can be done if necessary but not for the purpose of allowing management to fill up a lacuna left by Presenting Officer or to disadvantage of Delinquent Officer or to cause serious prejudice or to give an unfair advantage to the Presenting Officer. Thus, additional evidence should not be received under disguise for changing nature of charges. Re-examination should not be made a tool for wiping out an admission of the witness.

## Written Briefs

Conduct Regulations generally provides that Inquiring Authority may permit the parties to file written briefs of their respective cases. In a case where Delinquent Officer while concluding his defense stated that he did not intend to say anything further provided no written briefs are filed by Presenting Officer, which if done, should be brought to his notice in order to enable him to tender the counter statement, if required but Inquiring Authority gave two days time to file briefs to both the parties and no written brief was filed by Presenting Officer. Therefore, in such circumstances, there is no question of filing of written briefs by Delinquent Officer.[1] Actually, written briefs are relatable to the cases of the party concerned. In other words, the written brief should contain what is the case of the party. There is no requirement that written briefs should be filed one after another. It is not required that one party has to wait till filing of written brief by the other.

1. Debotosh Pal Choudhry Vs Punjab National Bank and Others 2003(1) Bank CLR 654 (S.C.)

# CHAPTER 7

# DEFENCE IN INQUIRY

1. **Defense Representative**
2. **Representation by a Lawyer in Disciplinary Action/Proceedings**

Stage for defense in Inquiry starts from the very beginning of the inquiry itself. After management has presented its case and all evidences which are countered by the defense stagewise have been put on the record of the inquiry, the case of management is over and now defense has the right to bring on record its evidence apart from what has been tendered in the inquiry previously. The evidence in defense will be either documentary or oral. It should be kept in mind that it is the management who has to prove its case based upon the charge-sheet and no duty is cast upon to the Delinquent Officer to prove his innocence or to disprove the charges leveled against him. It will depend upon the facts of each case whether any evidence in defense is required or not. While circumstances warrant and indicate the need to lay any defense evidence, such evidence has to be brought by the defense on the record of inquiry. To tender evidence in defense is a right available to the Delinquent Officer. Therefore, it is for the defense to choose either to exercise this right to tender evidence or choose not to exercise it. Merely because the management has examined a number of witnesses or a heap of documents is produced, it is not necessary for the defense to produce any evidence or to examine any witness. It is not the quantity of evidence that matters but it is the quality of evidence that is to say the factual nature of evidence that will be the guiding factor.

Actually, defense evidence is not a substantive piece of evidence in itself. This is evidence in rebuttal. There may be need in some inquiries to let in defense evidence for the specific purpose of countering the evidence tendered by management's witness. Therefore, the scope of defense evidence is very limited. Accordingly, whenever defense intends to introduce any particular document as defense exhibit in the Inquiry

Proceedings, care has to be taken to ensure that the document does not go in any way to the adverse of the interest of the Delinquent Officer. The contents of the document proposed to be brought as defense exhibit should be carefully analysed in order to find out whether the same can be utilised by the management in proving the case against the Delinquent Officer. Similar will be the case with the examination of defense witness.

Therefore, the only guiding factor for producing any evidence on the part of the defense will be whether there is any need for any additional evidence in rebuttal and whether there is any reason for the defense to produce any witness.

The witnesses produced by the defense should be relevant and competent witnesses. They must have personal knowledge of the matters about which they are tendering evidence before the Inquiring Authority. The defense could therefore choose only such witnesses who are really competent witnesses and whose testimony cannot be successfully attacked by the Presenting Officer. The defense witness should be able to come out with irrefutable statements of facts. A defense witness should be able to stand the stress and strains of the cross-examination. The tenor of their evidence should be helpful and favourable to the defense. The defense witness should be capable of giving clear-cut reply with precision and accuracy. A witness who talks too much is a bad witness. If the reply to a question can be given in two words, the third word might prove to be harmful and dangerous. If there are several defense witnesses, care should be taken to ensure that they do not contradict with each other and that the evidence of all such witnesses is cogent in relation to the facts. There must be proper collaboration and harmony between the several witnesses produced by the defense. A defense witness should have a proper understanding of the charges and the facts which they are going to state as witness. A defense witness in his overanxiety to assist the Delinquent Officer should not come out with illogical or absurd answers. His testimony should be logical and cogent and related to facts which can be established. A defense witness can be cross-examined by the Presenting Officer with the same latitude as is available to defense while cross-examining management's witness. After understanding the factors as above said, a defense should select the witness to tender oral evidence. Since management cannot hope to prove the charges by cross-examination of the witness, the Presenting Officer has to prove his case through his own evidence that is to say through the management's exhibits and witness examined in support of the charges. An Inquiring Authority though cannot make a penetrating cross-examination but it is open to him to question the Delinquent Officer broadly and generally in relation to the evidence already on record of the inquiry.

## 1. DEFENSE REPRESENTATIVE

The opportunity of hearing necessarily implies that one must be able to present his case but the law in our country does not concede an absolute right of representation to an employee in domestic enquiry as part of his right to be heard and that there is no right to representation by somebody else unless the rules or regulations or standing orders, if any, regulating the conduct of Disciplinary Action/

Proceedings specifically recognise such a right and provide for such representation. Irrespective of desirability or otherwise, of giving the employee an opportunity facing charges of misconduct in a Disciplinary Action/Proceedings, to ensure that his defense does not get debilitated due to the inexperience or personal embarrassments, it cannot be claimed as a matter of right and that too as constituting an element of principles of natural justice to assert that a denial thereon would vitiate the enquiry itself.[1]

In pursuance to instructions of Government of India issued on the basis of suggestion emanating from the Central Vigilance Commission in consultation with Reserve Bank of India and amendment was made in relevant Conduct Regulation of Public Sector Bank of the effect that the officer employee shall not take the assistance of any other employee who has two pending disciplinary cases in hand in which he has to give assistance. This new provision has ensured that no monopoly is created in a chosen few. The above Regulation also operates as a clear bar against engagement of a legal practitioner unless Disciplinary Authority permits so. The right to representation is available only to the extent specifically provided or in the Rules of the Bank.

However, in banks, Conduct Regulations generally permits for engagement of Defense Representative also called as Assisting Officer. Though generally the management of Bank permits the Delinquent Officer to select Assisting Officer of his choice, yet the Delinquent Officer does not have or Conduct Regulations does not contemplate for such a right unfettered or absolute. Where bank was not able to spare the Assisting Officer/Defense Representative nominated by the Delinquent Officer for administrative reasons, the Delinquent Officer has to choose any other officer as his Assisting Officer/Defense Representative.[2]

## 2. REPRESENTATION BY A LAWYER IN DISCIPLINARY ACTION/PROCEEDINGS

Normally, a lawyer has no place in a disciplinary inquiry. But when the Presenting Officer, even if he is not a lawyer, is one who is well trained in prosecution work and if the Delinquent Officer cannot have the services of a legally trained person and is allowed only to have the services of a colleague who in the normal course will not be well versed in the subject, it goes without saying that will be nothing but denial of an opportunity to defend. Therefore, where the Presenting Officer is CBI Inspector and there is denial for appointment of lawyer for the employee, the penalty was set aside.[3]

Where grievance of the employee is that he has been pitted against a trained prosecutor but Disciplinary Authority brushed aside his request on the ground that Presenting Officer is not a legal practitioner, the refusal by Disciplinary Authority was considered bad.[4]

---

1. Indian Overseas Bank Vs Indian Overseas Bank Officers' Association and Another 2002(1) Bank CLR 55 2002(1) Bank CLR 74 (ORI)
2. Siva Prasad Vs State Bank of Travancore 2001(2) Bank CLR 105 (Kerala)
3. Union of India Vs Karunakaran Nayar 1986(1) Labour Law Judgment 124 (D.B.) (Kerala)
4. C.I. Subrahmaniam Vs Collector of Customs Cochin 1972(1) Labour Law Judgment 465

Similarly, where charges run into twenty-five pages and several hundreds of documents were involved, it was held that the Delinquent Officer will not be able to put forth his defense effectively without the assistance of a lawyer and accordingly, the writ was allowed.[1]

In Conduct Regulations of some banks, there is specific prohibition for appointment of legal practitioner to act as Defense Representative. In such cases also, Disciplinary Authority has to consider firstly the statutory prescription governing the procedure and secondly the sufferings or some prejudice by the Delinquent Officer. It is an option under Conduct Regulation given to Bank. The real test will be the test of prejudice as laid down by the Supreme Court.[2] Where charge is of abusing the superiors and assault of them, there do not exist any complicated questions of fact or laws because the employee himself will be the best person to throw light as to correctness of the allegations and he cannot be permitted for engagement of legal practitioner.[3] While appointing legal practitioner to be a Presenting Officer, Disciplinary Authority should ask the Delinquent Officer, if he so desires or wants to be defended by a defense assistant who is a legal practitioner.

Where Defense Representative selected by the Delinquent Officer refused to appear on behalf of the Delinquent Officer on the ground that they will not be able to spare two days in a week as the inquiry has been fixed for two days in every week, it was held that it cannot be ground for engaging him a legal practitioner in inquiry.[4]

## Role of Assisting Officer

Defense in any Disciplinary Action/Proceedings is not only technical job but a job of alertness and labour. Punishment to the Delinquent Officer always brings disgrace to Assisting Officer. Therefore, personal involvement up to a certain extent is desirable on the part of Assisting Officer. An inquiry cannot be defended like accomplishing a routine work in the office. To maintain equilibrium during the inquiry is hard toiling particularly when the mind of the Delinquent Officer is agitated and the world is seeing him with stern eyes. Therefore, smooth running of inquiry in a desired way is to be achieved by striking a nice balance amongst the various conflicting forces.

One reason for providing the facility of an Assisting Officer under the Conduct Regulation appears that the Delinquent Officer in his prevailing mental state of affairs cannot be or may not be able to put his case in a proper manner before the Inquiring Authority and this aspect should be appreciated considering the psychological pressure which a Delinquent Officer has to face during the inquiry.

---

1. G.V. Aswathanarayana Vs Central Bank of India, Bombay and Others 1993(2) Bank CLR 250
2. State Bank of Patiala Vs S.K. Sharma 1996 (II) Labour Law Judgment 296, 1996 (2) Bank CLR 59 (S.C.), 1996 Bankers' Journal 447 (S.C.), Judgment Today 1996(3) (S.C.) 722
3. K.M. Bhatt Vs Regional Manager, Dena Bank and Another 1998(1) Bank CLR 275
4. Chandra Prakash Gupta Vs Nideshak Kshetriya Gramin Bank and Others 2006(1) Bank CLR 1 (Allahabad)

Requirement of the job for Assisting Officer is to behave and have cordial and friendly atmosphere during inquiry but this has to be maintained without sacrificing the rights of the Delinquent Officer in any manner.

Management has not only enormous powers in relation to its employees but means also. There is a full-fledged system in support of the management while performing various Acts starting from preliminary investigation to punishment of the Delinquent Officer. Every corner of management is well secured and equipped with high sophisticated tools of working and staff while on the other side only Assisting Officer is there and incomplete or depressed help of the Delinquent Officer and in this background and state of affairs, the job of Assisting Officer is to bring the Delinquent Officer unscratched out of the inquiry.

Maintaining of high morals during the inquiry is the key for defending an inquiry properly. The onerous task is cast upon the Assisting Officer when charges are framed frivolously or concocted maliciously to satisfy the ego of some executive or to settle scores by way of vengeance.

No doubt, irregularities are there but it is also the part of the system. Fact remains that many go escort free though they should also be facing inquiry or they should not be in the Institution. Therefore, instead of fault-finding attitude with the Delinquent Officer, the job of the Assisting Officer is to lean towards the Delinquent Officer and opinion of Assisting Officer should always be favouring the Delinquent Officer not only personally but an effort should be made amongst the corners of the management to spread and create an atmosphere of congeniality and sympathy for the Delinquent Officer.

Discussions with experts may bring a more deep insight of many untouched aspects of the inquiry. Therefore, an Assisting Officer should never hesitate in discussing the pros and cons with such persons who are expert and experienced in the field.

Summing up, if an Assisting Officer is not convinced about the innocence of the Delinquent Officer, he should not offer himself for the job.

The purpose of Disciplinary Action/Proceedings is to bring to light the truth but truth is always as we perceive. If a Delinquent Officer considers himself guilty, there is no need for him for facing the inquiry; the simple course will be to make an admission of guilt. Therefore, the only truth which can be perceived by the Assisting Officer is innocence of the Delinquent Officer.

With above background in mind, an Assisting Officer should make the Delinquent Officer comfortable with himself and this is to be achieved by allowing and encouraging the Delinquent Officer to speak out and to hear the same with genuine interest and required patience.

At the time of engagement, Assisting Officer should clarify his duties which he is going to perform during the inquiry to the Delinquent Officer and Delinquent Officer's apprehension should be erased in a convincing manner and thus the stress level should be reduced to an extent where wisdom prevails instead of anxiety and worry.

Eligibility for doing the job of an Assisting Officer can be traced to the fact that Assisting Officer must be well acquainted with the procedure and norms of inquiry as well as about the matter to which the inquiry relates. Intricacies of the issues should be clear to him so that the finer points may be highlighted during the inquiry. Genuine sympathy and soft behaviour is the key for taking out correct information from the Delinquent Officer though never a guarantee of acquittal should be given by the Assisting Officer yet assurance should be given wholeheartedly. Assisting Officer need not to disclose his own thinking and chain of thoughts at every stage of matter because with the progress of the inquiry new issues and new defenses crop up and any unnecessary disclosure or conclusion may cause agitation in the mind of the Delinquent Officer. Further, the strategy disclosed may result in its failure. Therefore, an Assisting Officer will be well advised to be cautious in off-the-record conversation even.

## Tips for Assisting Officer

- Assisting Officer should always keep a copy of Conduct Rules, under which inquiry is being conducted, with himself alongwith the file of the case. Further, while being careful to take with the relevant files of the case at every hearing, however insignificant that hearing may be, the whole inquiry records is to be maintained in four files, to enable him to have a quick glance at any document, in case of need:

  (a) Disciplinary Action/Proceedings file strictly in chronological order;

  (b) Management witness' evidence/documents file;

  (c) Defense documents/witness file (if any); and

  (d) Important and confidential papers file (if any)

- The Delinquent Officer should always be accompanied by Assisting Officer while at the time of inspection of documents/files.
- The Delinquent Officer should be guided properly regarding how to reply before Inquiring Authority during mandatory questions or other questions.
- All the correspondence, documents should be signed by the Delinquent Officer himself. Only in case of need, Assisting Officer should sign.
- Have the patience of a bagger and never allegate Inquiring Authority of bias or otherwise in the proceedings out of rage and frustration. Charge of bias always prejudices Inquiring Authority to an extent if the same is unfounded. Unless there is truth in the allegations of bias, it is not advisable to make such allegations. An Assisting Officer has to mould himself so that Inquiring Authority can be handled properly. In avoiding the allegations of bias, the second point lies in the fact that the next Inquiring Authority will be more hard, more trained and more experienced. However, in case of real apprehension, no hesitation should be in bringing the truth to the light.

- An Assisting Officer should be very careful while recording the objections and they should not be presented in such a manner which puts the question mark on the competency of the Inquiring Authority. The Assisting Officer should choose the time of objection which he intends to raise and should also always weigh which irregularities under inquiry should be allowed to go on so that the same can be challenged at an appropriate stage. Suppose an opportunity to cross-examine the witness is not given then only a half line protest may be sufficient because it has vitiated the inquiry and its true impact may be highlighted at any appropriate stage like written brief etc. And thus instead of making continuous objection on the point, it will be proper to bring on record how prejudice has been caused to the Delinquent Officer so that the point may be fatal for the inquiry.
- Homework and skillful knowledge will provide an edge to the Assisting Officer before Inquiring Authority. Therefore, Disciplinary Action/ Proceedings should be attended after doing the necessary studies of the issues involved.
- To handle adjournments is one of the difficult tasks under inquiry. Inquiring Authority is always under pressure for early completion of the inquiry. Adjournments are of two kinds. Firstly, necessitated by the unexpected happening of an event where there is little role to be played by the Assisting Officer. Secondly, adjournments which are planned to carry out certain strategies. Inquiring Authority working in a time schedule may not give the desired period of time because that may cause agitation in the higher echelons of the management. Still there may be cooperation otherwise by the Inquiring Authority by understanding the difficulties of the party. Strategically, adjournments may have many purposes like bringing stay order from Court or for awaiting disposal of some representation or disposal of a verbal approach made to management. Such adjournments are difficult to get as a matter of fact and while seeking such adjournments it should always be remembered that granting of adjournments may go against the Delinquent Officer at some later stage. Therefore, suggestive course will be to take long adjournments with assurance to Inquiring Authority or Disciplinary Authority that further adjournment will not be taken.
- An Inquiring Authority should not be misleaded. Credibility of an Assisting Officer should be above board. Though it does not mean that Assisting Officer should disclose his defense or should cure the defects of the management's case, yet the separate personality of Assisting Officer has to be maintained without intermingling the same with that of the Delinquent Officer. Truthfulness and cordiality will always pay.
- Whenever Assisting Officer has an opportunity to interact with Presenting Officer or witnesses, he must do so.

# CHAPTER 8

# INQUIRING AUTHORITY AND ITS REPORT

1. **Evaluation and Appreciation of Evidence**
2. **Inquiry Report: (a) Furnishing of Inquiry Report to the Delinquent Officer**

In sum and substance, free and fair inquiry is the primary duty of Inquiring Authority which provides a reasonable opportunity to defend to the Delinquent Officer **and impartial findings** on the issues. The Inquiring Authority, therefore, should be a person with open mind frame. Although he is not a judicial authority as such, he should display judicial spirit in his actions.

Procedure for conducting of an inquiry is lengthy and complicated. Still it is expected that the same should be followed as closely as possible so that the inquiry may not be quashed by higher authorities or under judicial review. The broad principles which should be kept in mind by an Inquiring Authority are—

- There is no breach of the 'principles of natural justice.'
- There is no lack of jurisdiction or absence of authority.
- There is no faulty procedure.
- There is no bad faith in holding inquiry.

Inquiring Authority is also an appointee of the Disciplinary Authority. Inquiring Authority has to examine the charge and evidences tendered in support of charge and then to find out the truth regarding the allegations in the charge-sheet. Though conducting inquiry is an administrative affair but it has to be performed in a quasi-judicial manner. Once Disciplinary Authority issues appointment letter for Inquiring

Authority, the role of Disciplinary Authority comes to an end and the job assigned to the Inquiring Authority is to submit its findings regarding the guilt to the Disciplinary Authority. Therefore, though an Inquiring Authority may be subordinate to the Disciplinary Authority in the hierarchy of system, but the job of inquiry is not subordinate to the Disciplinary Authority and an Inquiring Authority cannot act on the dictates of Disciplinary Authority or any other official in the system. The Inquiring Authority should not only be fair and neutral to the parties concerned but also appear to be so.

Inquiring Authority performs a quasi-judicial function. The charges leveled against the Delinquent Officer must be found to have been proved. The Inquiring Authority has a duty to arrive at findings upon taking into consideration the materials brought on record by the parties. He cannot travel beyond the charges. Inquiring Authority cannot inquire into the allegations with which Delinquent Officer is not charged with unless the same is provided/permitted in Conduct Regulations. Inquiring Authority cannot take into consideration any irrelevant fact. He cannot refuse to consider the relevant fact. Inquiring Authority cannot shift the burden of proof.

Admission of guilt or of the charges by the Delinquent Officer has to be recorded by the Inquiring Authority in such a manner so that the same may be sufficient to complete the proving of the charge and if not the Inquiry has to be carried out. He has to judge whether the admissions which are being made before him are not coming out due to any coercion, fraud or undue pressure and the same are made by the Delinquent Officer on his own free will. An Inquiring Authority should make himself well conversant with the provisions of Conduct Regulations of the Bank providing rules for inquiry and should try to adhere to the same scrupulously. An Inquiring Authority should not/cannot import his personal knowledge of the facts under Disciplinary Action/Proceedings even if there is any possibility of the kind, he should inform the management of his involvement in the matter so that management can withdraw the inquiry from him.

In case of objection by either side, Inquiring Authority has to give its ruling in an unbiased manner and should also give necessary justification for disposal of the objection in a particular way. Inquiring Authority should be careful that at no stage of inquiry there arise a scope for the Delinquent Officer to allege bias and denial of justice.

The Supreme Court has held[1] that an Inquiring Authority need not be an officer of the Bank as even a third party can be appointed as Inquiring Authority.

Inquiring Authority should act impartially, objectively and without bias, keeping in mind the proverb "justice must not only be done but it must also appear to have been done."

1. Central Bank of India Vs C. Barnard 1991(1) S.C.C. 319, 1991(1) Bank CLR 311 (S.C.)

Apart from these, following practical tips may be as under—

- 'Principles of natural justice' should be given top priority. An extra opportunity in case of doubt is better than no opportunity to the Delinquent Officer. Follow the 'principles of natural justice' not only in letter but in spirit also.
- On receipt of the appointment letter as Inquiring Authority from Disciplinary Authority, the same should be examined and in case of any mistake the same may be pointed out immediately. It is to be noted that defect in appointment may make the whole Inquiry Proceedings worthless.
- The charge-sheet should be examined and if there is incompleteness or error, the same should be pointed out. Once an inquiry is started, the Inquiring Authority need not to ask again the Delinquent Officer to state his defense.
- In nationalised banks, the practice has been to record the proceedings in verbatim. At the end of the day, all the members should be required to sign the last page as also initial on each of the Proceedings sheet. In case if anybody wants to go through the record of the Proceedings of the date, the same may be allowed.
- Deposition of witnesses may be recorded either in narrative form, or in question-answer form.
- In case the Delinquent Officer asks for copies of certain documents, Inquiring Authority will examine the relevancy of such documents in relation to the subject-matter of the charge for the purpose of his defense and will direct the concerned Authority in whose custody the documents are lying for providing an inspection/copies of the documents to the Delinquent Officer.
- On start of the actual hearing, Inquiring Authority would advice the Presenting Officer to present the management's case in support of the charges.
- Proceedings of inquiry once commenced should be carried out on day-to-day basis unless some particular stage is crossed. Mutual convenience of the parties though could be a considerable factor while fixing the next date but should not result in inordinate delay. Meaning thereby merits in respects of request for adjournments/postponements etc. should be carefully examined and unless genuine may not be agreed upon.
- It is the duty of the Inquiring Authority to provide an opportunity of cross-examination of the witnesses to the other party particularly the Delinquent Officer should be provided an opportunity for cross-examination of the management's witnesses. After completion of the cross-examination, Presenting Officer may be permitted to re-examine the witness on points raised during the cross-examination. Generally, under re-examination, no

new issues can be taken by the Presenting Officer because the purpose of re-examination is to clarify the ambiguities arising out of cross-examination.

- The testimonies of the witnesses should be recorded carefully so that there cannot be misinterpretation of any statement afterwards leading the case from field to granary.
- Once documents/witnesses from both sides have been led, before conclusion of the proceedings, an opportunity should be granted to the Delinquent Officer to make or state his defense orally or in writing as the Delinquent Officer may prefer. If statement of defense is made orally, it shall be recorded and the Delinquent Officer should be required to sign the record. Needless to say, if it is in writing, it must be signed. Copy of such statement of defense should be provided to Presenting Officer as a matter of course.
- If the Delinquent Officer has not got himself examined or has not made any statement of defense after closing of the evidence, Inquiring Authority may generally question him on the circumstances peeping out of the evidence.
- On conclusion of the Disciplinary Action/Proceedings, the Inquiring Authority will call for written briefs from the parties. Though under Conduct Regulations, Presenting Officer may not be required to submit the same yet Inquiring Authority has ample powers to call for the same for a just decision of the matter or verbal briefs can also be sought.
- An Inquiring Authority should understand its role and responsibilities while conducting inquiry from the stage of his appointment till the time of delivery of findings provided the power of a fair inquiry giving undaunted discretion. Mere wild allegations should not be encouraged inasmuch as that will tend to subvert smooth functioning of Disciplinary Action/Proceedings.

## 1. EVALUATION AND APPRECIATION OF EVIDENCE BY INQUIRING AUTHORITY

While reaching to the final conclusion or preparing the Inquiry Report, an Inquiring Authority has to take cognizance of all the evidences brought on record. Word 'Evidence' means and includes:

Firstly, all statements of witness is in relation to matters of facts under inquiry (oral evidence).

Secondly, all documents including electronic records (audio, video and computer CD, pen drive or like any other device) produced for inspection of Inquiring Authority (called documentary evidence).

The stage of evidence starts when the charge-sheet is served to the Delinquent Officer. Then question arises what evidence will be relevant for the purpose of Inquiring Authority and how the Authority will decide the relevancy of evidence in relation to the charges.

Relevancy of evidence depends upon several factors and the same cannot be codified fully. However, in general, following evidences may be said to be relevant.

(a) When evidence pertains to *'fact in issue',* it means any fact from which either by itself or in connection with some other fact, the existence, non-existence nature or extent of any right, liability or disability asserted or denied in the proceedings necessarily follows. In Disciplinary Action/ Proceedings, misconduct of the Delinquent Officer is the *fact in issue.*

(b) When evidence pertains to any other or allied fact which is a relevant fact otherwise including—

(i) When other fact is so connected with *fact in issue* so as to form part of same transaction regardless of the fact they occurred at the same time and place or at different times and places.

(ii) Facts which are the occasion, cause or effect, immediate or otherwise, of relevant facts or *facts in issue* or which constitutes the state of things under which they happened or which afforded an opportunity for their occurrence or transaction will be relevant.

(iii) Any fact is relevant which shows or constitute a motive or preparation for any *fact in issue* or for relevant fact. It is noticeable that motive is not an important part in Disciplinary Action/Proceedings expect in the cases of insubordinacy or where there may be an existence of motive for doing a particular misconduct. It is not the duty of management to prove the motive. The management has to prove only the misconduct as alleged. In cases of disobedience, the same may be deliberate and intentional and for that it is to be proved that the Delinquent Officer was in a position to obey the instructions of his superior. The motive may reduce the degree of misconduct when Delinquent Officer put forward his evidence of the effect that he was having no motive to disobey the superiors.

(iv) Fact necessary to explain or introduce a *fact in issue* (misconduct) or relevant fact or which support or rebut an inference suggested by a fact in issue (misconduct) or relevant fact or which establishes the identity of any thing or person or fix the time and place at which any *fact in issue* (misconduct) or relevant fact happened.

(v) Fact, not otherwise relevant, still will be relevant if they support or are inconsistent with the opinions of the experts when such opinions are relevant.

(vi) When Inquiring Authority/Disciplinary Authority has to form an opinion as to the person by whom any document was written or signed, the opinion of any person acquainted with the handwriting of the person by whom it is supposed to be written or signed that it was or was not written or signed by that person will be a relevant fact.

The next question is as to *burden of proof.* Generally, the burden of proof in any Proceedings lies on the party who would fail if no evidence at all were given on either side. Since management has launched the Disciplinary Action/Proceedings for taking a decision on the alleged misconduct of the Delinquent Officer, it is but natural that burden of proof will be on management for proving the facts of articles of charge-sheet. For proper evaluation of evidence, it is necessary for Inquiring Authority to apply the principle of burden of proof by calling the management to lead the evidence for substantiating the allegations.

There *is no burden of proof on the Delinquent Officer* to prove his innocence, still there are many exceptions to this general rule like when a Delinquent admits the guilt and plead some extenuating circumstances then burden will be shifted to him. Throwing of burden of proof upon the management is in consonance with the principles of natural justice.

Further, while appreciating and evaluating the evidence under inquiry, the Inquiring Authority has to take some matter/positions as granted. Certain presumptions are to be drawn in order to cut down evidence so that real issue may not be oversighted. Though there cannot be any exhaustive list of such presumptions, yet we give some of those as under —

- That person who was involved in the misconduct himself is unworthy of credit.
- That Bank documents are genuine documents.
- That a thing or state of things which has been shown to be in existence within a period shorter than that within which such thing or state of things usually cease to exit is still in existence.
- All judicial and official acts are done in a regular way.
- That common course of business has been followed in a particular transaction/case.
- That evidence which could be and is not produced before the Inquiring Authority would if produced be unfavourable to the party who withholds it. This is called "best evidence rule" and management has to produce all the relevant evidence to the charges. Accordingly, when the Delinquent Officer took the plea of having acted on the oral instructions of branch manager and branch manager though was cited as management witness, did not turn up to rebut the allegations, it was held that preponderance of probability is in favour of Delinquent Officer and adverse inference can be drawn.[1]
- That if a man refuses to answer a question which he is not compelled to answer, the answer if given would be unfavourable to him.

---

1. Venkatarama Murlidhar Shenoy Vs Syndicate Bank 2001(2) Bank CLR 48 (Calcutta)

The above and other *presumptions are discretionary with Inquiring Authority to apply* and in case where facts and circumstances warrant for not raising such presumptions, the Inquiring Authority may refuse or in other words the presumptions can be rebutted by cogent and sufficient evidence.

Having discussed about the facts, now we will discuss various types of evidence which an Inquiring Authority has to evaluate while reaching to conclusions or giving its findings.

## Documentary Evidence

As per Indian Evidence Act, the documentary evidence can be of two types, one primary (original) evidence, and the other secondary evidence.

It is only in specified cases the secondary evidences can be produced in Court.[1] However, this rule cannot be applied as it is in Disciplinary Action/Proceedings. because Disciplinary Action/Proceedings are in-house proceedings and being part and parcel Inquiring Authority of the Institution has to be more informal and direct. Therefore, when management produces copies of correspondence, circulars etc., the same cannot be discarded by Inquiring Authority without any cogent reason. Official circulars, letters, photos, complaint, data, registers, computer sheets are the documentary évidence through which the management proves its defense.

## Oral Evidence

Oral evidence is a deposition made by the witnesses. Oral evidence will be either in support of document/paper/writings etc. or may be in respect of witnessing particular evidence. We will discuss the full impact of these evidences elsewhere.

Now, question arises how the evidence will be evaluated by Inquiring Authority. Evidence has to be tested on many scores and accordingly the same will be given credence in proving the charges. An Inquiring Authority while evaluating evidence must understand its true impact as well as its real value.

---

1. Section 65 of Evidence Act: Cases in which secondary evidence relating to documents may be given —

   Secondary evidence may be given of the existence, condition or contents of a document in the following cases:

   (a) When the original is in possession or power (i) of the opposite party; or (ii) of the person who is out of the reach of, or not subject to, the process of the Court, or (iii) of any person legally bound to produce it, and when such person does not produce it after demand, i.e., notice under Section 66;

   (b) When the existence or condition or contents of the original are admitted in writing by the person against whom it is proved;

   (c) When the original is lost or destroyed;

   (d) When its production is physically impossible or highly inconvenient;

   (e) When the original is public document;

   (f) When the original is a document of which a certified copy is permitted by this Act;

   (g) When the originals consist of numerous account or other documents which cannot conveniently be examined in Court. If the original document is lost, destroyed, detained by the opponent or third person who does not produce it after notice or is physically irremovable, secondary evidence is admissible."

## Direct Evidence and Hearsay Evidence

Evidence coming from the source itself that has been either eye witness or has concluded the things himself and any such document which is itself the proof of the misconduct is direct evidence which means all statements or declarations of persons not called as witnesses but represented by somebody else. Literally, it means evidence of a person who has heard from another. Such type of evidence is admissible in Inquiry because it is not always possible to produce direct evidence and being official acts and witnesses, also being officials of the institutions, there remains *prima facie* good reason to believe such evidence.

## Circumstantial Evidence

When no direct evidence is available, a fact can be proved by the number of surrounding circumstances provided they lead to point to the fact in issue or relevant fact. In cases of fraud, particularly circumstantial evidences is the only evidence, because culprit does not leave traces of fraud leading to him and it is only circumstantial evidence which may point towards the perpetrator of fraud.

## Evaluation of Admission Regarding Misconduct

In so many cases, the Delinquent Officers often admit their guilt/irregularities. Where an admission is clear-cut and unambiguous, the Disciplinary Authority is entitled to proceed by dispensing with the inquiry. No evidence needs to be lead. But evidence is always required to prove disputed facts and doubtful facts.

Admissions regarding guilt can be made by the Delinquent Officer at two stages—

Firstly, at the stage of preliminary investigation or before issue of charge-sheet.

Secondly, after issue of charge-sheet before Inquiring Authority/Disciplinary Authority.

So far as question of admissions made before issuing charge-sheet are concerned, they are to be considered by the Disciplinary Authority.

Unless a statement of Delinquent Officer leads to a clear and unambiguous admission of his guilt, failure to hold a formal inquiry would certainly constitute serious infirmity because under the Conduct Regulations of Bank a charge-sheeted officer is entitled for hearing. Even where Disciplinary Authority has not conducted/ordered for an inquiry and an order of punishment is passed, on the basis of admission Disciplinary Authority has to record its findings and procedure of Service Regulations of Bank has to be followed seriously.

Thus, where the Delinquent Officer after admitting of shortage of case, made good the shortage, order of removal was passed by holding that there is temporary misappropriation by employee, the order was treated bad as charge of embezzlement was a new charge and employee never admitted temporary misappropriation[1] of the

1. Allahabad Bank Vs Pronab Kumar Mukherjee and Others 1993(2) Bank CLR 67

funds of Bank but admitted only shortage of cash. Similarly, where Inquiring Authority submitted his report considering the admissions in words " ..... *I could not submit a conclusive report especially with regard to charges I and XVI due to counter charges and counter statements which need further inquiry as already stated while dealing with the relative charges..* " and Disciplinary Authority proceeded to award punishment of dismissal it was held[1] that order passed is without proper inquiry.

As far as admission after issue of charge-sheet or during inquiry are concerned, we may say that if the Delinquent Officer accepts the guilt in respect of the charges leveled voluntary and unequivocal terms, there will be no need to conduct inquiry further and Inquiring Authority after considering the acceptance of the guilt by the Delinquent Officer, can send a report without examining the witness or without considering the other material and document. Based on the findings of the Inquiring Authority's report, appropriate action will be taken by the Disciplinary Authority. The entire statement made by the Delinquent Officer must be considered *in toto* to come to the conclusion that such statement amounts to admission of guilt.

However, when the Inquiring Authority merely on the basis of a vague statement made by the Delinquent Officer or considering only a part of the statement, without taking the statement *in toto* in account comes to the conclusion that Delinquent Officer had admitted the guilt and on such a footing proceeds without conducting further inquiry to make a report finding the Delinquent Officer guilty of charges, the inquiry will not be a fair inquiry in the eye of law.

If an employee makes admission of guilt by the endorsement of investigation report and secondly, during the course of inquiry there is no need for Inquiring Authority to record evidence.[2]

Similarly, a confession made by an accused in criminal case though may not be admissible in that case in view of Sections 25 and 27 of Indian Evidence Act; still that Confessional statement is admissible in Disciplinary Action/Proceedings.[3]

However if the Delinquent Officer has been discharged in criminal proceedings despite such confession, Inquiring Authority should take into consideration the discharge order which is based on self same evidence.[4]

**Evaluation of evidence to prove motive:** It is not the duty of management to prove the motive. The management has to prove the misconduct alleged. However, if the charge is that there was disobedience, then it has to be proved that disobedience was deliberate and intentional for that it is to be proved that the employee was in a position to obey his superior. Since the motive reduces the degree of misconduct for that the employee concerned has to put forward his evidence stating that he also had no motive to disobey the superior.

---

1. The Nagarjuna Grameena Bank Khammans and Another Vs M.P. Bruce 1995(2) Bank CLR 501 (A.P.)
2. P.K. Thakanchan Vs Thalandu Service Co-operative Bank Ltd. and Another 1994(1) Bank CLR 404
3. Commissioner of Police, New Delhi Vs Narendra Singh 2006(4) S.C.C. 265
4. Roop Singh Negi Vs Punjab National Bank 2009(1) Bank CLR 510 (S.C.)

**Evaluation of evidence in Alibi:** Where the defense takes plea that when a particular incident took place he was not at the scene, in such cases, the employee concerned has to substantiate by producing evidence that he was not at the scene, where he was, if he was at his residence he may produce his family members or other persons which may be subject to cross-examination.

**Evaluation of evidence to prove provocation:** The provocation also reduces the degree of offence but the burden is always on the Delinquent Officer. If the provocation took place because of verbal indecent remark passed by the superior or co-worker which resulted into a physical assault by the Delinquent Officer, no doubt verbal indecent remarks can be condemned but at the same time it may not absolve the Delinquent Officer from the gravity of misconduct and the misconduct stands proved. The dismissal of an employee on such count is upheld by the Court. Here again, the onus is on the Delinquent Officer to prove that he was provoked.

**Evaluation of evidence in respect of Superior's instructions:** Such defense has to be taken up at the very first stage of the Proceedings and if superior's instructions are given by an authority verbally or otherwise are beyond his powers, the defense cannot succeed.

**Evaluation of evidence in respect of negligence:** Negligence has to be proved by the management. But the Delinquent Officer can produce such evidence where it can be interpreted that he has taken every caution to safeguard the interest of the Institution and negligence was bonafide one while on the other hand, the management has to prove that every thing was in order and normal but only negligence caused the omission or commission of misconduct.

**Evaluation of evidence in corroboration:** It means further strengthening the evidence already adduced. Documentary evidence can be corroborated by witnesses and witnesses can be corroborated by other witnesses. Corroborating evidence is not necessary but is adduced a view of the best evidence rule. Its evaluation is always done with the evidence to which it corroborates.

**Evaluation of evidence of handwriting and signature:** Handwriting and signature can be confirmed in the following ways—

(a) By calling the person who has written or signed himself.

(b) By calling the person in whose presence the document was written and signed.

(c) By calling the person who is acquainted with the writing and signature of the maker of the document and who can opine definitely.

(d) Handwriting expert who opines on the basis of the comparison between admitted writing and the disputed writing.

(e) Inquiring Authority can itself, being a banker, compare writing and signature.

## 2. INQUIRY REPORT

Findings of Inquiry or the Inquiry Report is the mirror and the face of the entire process which indicates whether proper care has been taken while imposing the penalty. Therefore, such findings/Inquiry Report have to be prepared with all seriousness and caution. After the inquiry is concluded and the written arguments/ briefs of the parties if any are received, the Inquiring Authority is required to record and submit his report and findings to the Disciplinary Authority. The Inquiring Authority is required to prepare a comprehensive report in the light of evidences and their evaluation as aforesaid containing his own reasoning for accepting or rejecting the evidences in record. However, his analysis will be confined to the charges leveled against the Delinquent Officer and to the material/evidences brought on record. Inquiring Authority has to prove or disprove the articles of charge specifically. The Inquiry Report has to be submitted within a reasonable time. Inquiring Authority has no business to suggest about punishment.

Submission of Inquiry Findings should be given in respect of each charge as Conduct Regulations of the Bank directs and should contain necessarily the following:

(i) Gist of the charge and the statement of imputation of misconduct.

(ii) Management's case as presented by Presenting Officer in support of the charge.

(iii) The gist of the evidences led by the management side. Here, the documentary evidences relied upon for each charge should be listed with description and relevance. There may be common exhibits for different charges. In such cases, the exhibits should be repeated for each charge. Likewise, the witnesses may give his deposition covering various charges. In such cases, the deposition relevant for a particular charge should be narrated under each charge. The gist of evidence led by defense in respect of each charge should be described in the aforesaid manner.

(iv) Defense argument.

(v) Inquiring Authority's assessment and analysis of evidence documentary as well as oral.

(vi) Whether the charge is proved or not and justification for the same.

Where Inquiry Report reveals that Inquiring Authority has taken pains to first deal with the statement of imputation of misconduct, secondly lapses/irregularities observed on the part of Delinquent Officer as submitted by the management, thirdly the detailed analysis of evidence adduced on behalf of management, fourthly the evidence adduced on behalf of the defense and lastly, the oral briefs, it cannot be said that Inquiring Authority has not applied its mind.[1] The Inquiring Authority is not supposed to record his findings on each and every allegation or imputation even if

---

1. Syndicate Bank Manipal Vs M.C. Bhatta (deceased) through LRs 1998(2) Bank CLR 419

some facts which are alleged in support of the charge are not held to be proved by evidence or record, what has to be seen is as to whether the charge in its general and composite form stands proved or not. It is the cumulative effect of the findings of Inquiring Authority as regards various facets that lead to finding as to whether charge is proved or not proved. The order of Inquiring Authority need not be written in the manner in which a judicial officer would write yet what one has to see, is whether the order is sufficiently clear and contains the reason in justification for the conclusions carried at absence of reason in a disciplinary order would amount to denial of natural justice.

Reasons are nothing but intellectual faculty by which conclusions are drawn from premises reaching conclusion by connected thought. It is a faculty of mind by which it distinguishes truth from falsehood, good from evil and which enable the possessor to deduce inference from fact and from preposition. The object underlined the rules of recording reasons is to prevent miscarriage of justice and to secure fair play in action.

Recording of reason requires coherent and logical thinking and drawing inference from conclusions by systematic analysis from facts known. Reasons are link between materials on which certain conclusions are based. They disclose how the mind is applied towards the subject-matter of decision. Reasons reveal the rational nexus between the facts considered and the conclusions reached. The reasons should demonstrate that there is logical and legal basis for their ultimate conclusions. The reasons provide means whereby a party is apprised of why a decision has been made.

An order silent render it impossible for higher authorities or for judicial review in adjudging the validity of decision. Right to reason is an indispensable part of a sound system. This is the salutory requirement of natural justice to spell out the reasons in the order made. In other words, a speaking out.

## (a) Furnishing of Inquiry Report to the Delinquent Officer

The implication of non-furnishing of the inquiry report is well known. It has been held by Supreme Court[1] that non-furnishing of Inquiry Report goes to the root of the matter and makes of impugned order of dismissal inoperative in the eye of law. The reason why the right to receive the report of the Inquiring Authority is considered an essential part of the reasonable opportunity at the first stage and also a principle of natural justice is that the findings recorded by the Inquiring Authority form an important material before the Disciplinary Authority which along with the evidence is taken into consideration by it in order to come to its conclusions. It is difficult to say in advance as to what extent the findings including the punishment, if any recommended in report would influence the Disciplinary Authority while drawing its conclusion.

1. Union of India Vs Mohammad Ramzan Khan A.I.R. 1991 S.C. 471, 1991(1) S.C.C page 588

The findings further might have been recorded by considering the relevant evidence on record, or by misconstruing it or unsupported by it. If such a finding is to be one of the documents to be considered by the Disciplinary Authority, the 'principles of natural justice' require that the employee should have a fair opportunity to meet, explain and controvert it before he is condemned. It is negation of the tenets of justice and a denial of fair opportunity to the employee to consider the findings recorded by a third party like the Inquiring Authority without giving the employee an opportunity to reply to it. Although it is true that the Disciplinary Authority is supposed to arrive at its own that the Disciplinary Authority takes into consideration on record.

Merely supplying a copy of Inquiry Report after passing of an order and affording an opportunity at appellate stage will not make difference as the Delinquent Officer has been kept away from the conclusions arrived at by Inquiring Authority and punishment has been inflected without bringing to the knowledge of the Delinquent Officer. Therefore, such order will be violative of 'natural justice'.[1] Later discussing the effect of Mohammad Ramzan case, Supreme Court[2] held as under:

*"..... The next question to be answered is what is the effect on the order of punishment when the report of the Inquiring Authority is not furnished to the employee and what relief should be granted to him in such cases. The answer to this question has to be relative to the punishment awarded.*

*When the employee is dismissed or removed from service and the inquiry is set aside because the report is not furnished to him, in such cases, the non-furnishing of the report may have prejudiced him gravely while in other cases it may have made no difference to the ultimate punishment awarded to him. Hence, to direct reinstatement of the employee with back wages in all cases to reduce the rules of justice to a mechanical ritual. The theory of reasonable opportunity and the principles of natural justice have been evolved to uphold the rule of law and to assist the individual to vindicate his just rights. They are not incantations to be invoked nor rates to be performed on all and sundry occasions. Whether in fact prejudice has been caused to the employee or not on account of the denial to him of the report, has to be considered on the fact and circumstances of each case. Where, therefore, even after the furnishing of the report, no different consequence would have followed, it would be a perversion of justice to permit the employee to resume duty and to get all the consequential benefits. It amounts to rewarding the dishonest and the guilty and thus a stretching the concept of justice to illogical and exasperating limits. It amounts to an 'unnatural expansion of natural justice' which in itself in unethical to justice."*

1. Baithyanath Shukla Vs Central Bank of India 1992(2) Bank CLR 473
2. Managing Director ECIL Vs B. Karunaker AIR 1994 S.C. 1074

*The procedure for furnishing copy of Inquiry Report* may be summarised as follows:

(i) If all the charges are held proved by the Inquiring Authority and the Disciplinary Authority agrees with the findings, he (Disciplinary Authority) will hand over a copy of findings to the Delinquent Officer intimating that the Disciplinary Authority agrees with the findings and that the Delinquent Officer may make his submissions against the said findings.

(ii) If some charges have been held as proved while some other are held as not proved and the Disciplinary Authority agrees with such findings, he will act in the same manner as is mentioned under point (i).

(iii) If the Disciplinary Authority holds some charges as proved and some not proved and Disciplinary Authority disagrees with the finding, in part the Disciplinary Authority will give his own reasons for disagreement in respect of the charges which have been held as not proved by Inquiring Authority. Disciplinary Authority will intimate the reasons alongwith a copy of findings and will advice the Delinquent Officer to make submissions on total findings.

(iv) Where the Inquiring Authority comes to the conclusion that all the charges are not proved and Disciplinary Authority agrees with such findings, there will be no need to send the copy of findings and to call for the submissions of the Delinquent Officer and Disciplinary Authority will pass final orders straightway.

In a case where Disciplinary Authority while disagreeing with the findings of Inquiring Authority did not provide an opportunity to show cause before passing of final orders of punishment, it was held[1] that Disciplinary Authority should have granted an opportunity before recording of his own findings and accordingly without considering the merits of the case, the matter was remitted to the Bank for consideration afresh.

1. A.K. Gaur Vs Central Bank of India 2001(2) Bank CLR 248 (Allahabad)

# CHAPTER 9

# DISCIPLINARY AUTHORITY AND PUNISHMENT

1. **Role of Vigilance Department**
2. **Role of Appellate Authority**
3. **Personal Hearing before Appellate Authority**

## DISCIPLINARY AUTHORITY

An inquiry can be conducted either by an Inquiring Authority or by a Disciplinary Authority itself in accordance with Conduct Regulations. When inquiry is conducted by the Inquiring Authority, his report/findings are not final or conclusive and the Disciplinary Action/Proceedings do not stand concluded. The Disciplinary Action/ Proceedings stand concluded with the decision of the Disciplinary Authority. It is the Disciplinary Authority who can impose penalty and not the Inquiring Authority. Where Disciplinary Authority conducts the inquiry, an opportunity of hearing is to be granted by him. In the case where Disciplinary Authority agrees with the findings of Inquiring Authority, it is not obligatory on the part of Disciplinary Authority to discuss the evidence and the facts and circumstances established at the departmental enquiry in detail and write as if it were an order or a judgment of a judicial Tribunal. If Disciplinary Authority agrees with the findings of Inquiring Authority that all the charges mentioned in the charge-sheet had been established, it means that he is affirming the findings on each charge and this would be satisfying the requirement of relevant regulation. When the Disciplinary Authority differs with the view of Inquiring Authority and proposes to come to a different conclusion, there is no reason why an opportunity of hearing should not be granted. Principles of natural justice have to be read into the Regulations of Bank. Disciplinary Authority should have regard to the principle that strict rules of evidence are not applicable to Disciplinary Action/ Proceedings. The requirement of law is that the allegations against the Delinquent Officer must be established by such evidence acting upon which a reasonable person acting reasonably and with objectivity may arrive at a finding upholding the charge. Conjecture and surmises should not be cause for sustaining the findings of guilt. Instead findings must be supported with evidence. A Disciplinary Authority will be well advised if it enquires whether there is any evidence to support the conclusion drawn in the findings of Inquiring Authority.

While finding that Regulation 7(2) of Punjab National Bank Officer Employee Discipline and Appeal Regulation 1977, is para materia (identical) to Rule 50(3)(ii) of State Bank of India (Supervisory Staff) Service Rules, Supreme Court[1] refused to accept the contention raised on behalf of management that unless it is shown that some prejudice was caused to the Delinquent Officer, the order of dismissal cannot be set aside by High Court in case where Disciplinary Authority while disagreed with the findings of Inquiry Report did not provide opportunity to the Delinquent Officer.

In plainer words, whenever the Disciplinary Authority disagrees with the Inquiring Authority on any Article of charge, then before it records its own findings on such charge, it must record its tentative reasons for such disagreement and give to the Delinquent Officer employee an opportunity to represent before it records findings.

The report of the Inquiring Authority containing its findings will have to be conveyed and the employee will have an opportunity to persuade the Disciplinary Authority to accept the favourable conclusion of the Inquiring Authority. The principles of natural justice require the authority which has to take the final decision and can impose the penalty, to give an opportunity to the employee charged of misconduct to file representation before Disciplinary Authority.[2] Where Inquiring Authority completely exonerated of the charges but without recording any reasons whatsoever as to why Disciplinary Authority in differing from his findings, the Disciplinary Authority passed the order of punishment as follows—

*"The penalty of reduction of his pay by one stage in time-scale of pay applicable to him be and is hereby imposed upon Shri S.P. Misra." The same was held illegal and quashed.*[3]

For one disciplinary inquiry against a concerned officer at a given point of time, there would be only one disciplinary authority. But that would not mean that the entire gamut of the departmental enquiry against the officer must be conducted from beginning to end by only one Disciplinary Authority and one competent Disciplinary Authority which initiated the proceedings cannot get changed in midstream by another

1. State Bank of India and Others Vs K.P. Narainan Kutty 2003(1) Bank CLR 401 (S.C.)
2. Punjab National Bank Vs Kunj Bihari Mishra 1998(2) Bank CLR 28 (S.C.), J.T 1998(5) S.C. 607, 1998(80) FLR 841 (S.C.)
3. Sharda Prasad Misra Vs Assistant General Manager, Union Bank of India Central Office, Personnel Department, Bombay 2000(3) Bank CLR 247 (Allahabad)

equally competent disciplinary authority.[1] Going further, the disciplinary authority of the erstwhile place of posting, where irregularities stated to have occurred/committed can institute and complete Disciplinary Action/Proceedings against the erring officials (both officers/award staff) notwithstanding the fact that such staff/officer are later posted under the administrative jurisdiction of some other authority. Where Bank in its wisdom felt that powers of specified authorities may be exercised by any other authorities nominated by executive director and managing director, who is equal in rank or higher than the authority specified in Regulations, the same cannot be questioned and such course of Bank management stands approved by Court.[2]

A non-official cannot act as a disciplinary authority and pass an order of punishment against the Delinquent Officer employee. Taking the above view, it was held that a retired employee cannot act as a disciplinary authority.[3] Where Conduct Regulations of Bank provided that Disciplinary Authority will be any DGM or any AGM, then it cannot be construed that where DGM has initiated Disciplinary Action/ Proceedings only he is entitled to carry out and pass final order and any order passed by AGM will be bad who has been appointed Disciplinary Authority at a later stage of inquiry.[4] A Disciplinary Authority has right to change its order though the same may have been come in black and white on its internal correspondence/office notes but not pronounced or communicated. When an order is made in an office noting in a file but is not pronounced, published or communicated, nothing prevents the authority from correcting it or altering for valid reasons. However, once the order is pronounced or communicated, the authority becomes ***functious offcio.***

It is always open to Disciplinary Authority to adopt the inquiry report or to differ from it. If the inference of fact is one which reasonable person would draw from the proved facts of the matter, the Court will not interfere.

Where there are some relevant materials which the authority has accepted and which material may reasonably support the conclusion that the employee is guilty, the Court will not review the material and will not arrive at an independent findings on the material available on the record of inquiry. If the inquiry has been properly held, the question of adequacy or reliability of the evidence cannot be canvassed before the Court. The Tribunal/Court also cannot interfere with the penalty if the conclusion of Inquiring Authority or the competent authority is based on evidence even if some of it is found to be irrelevant or extraneous to the matter.[5]

## PUNISHMENT

The integrity, trust and discipline from its employee are the very fundamentals of the Banking Industry. The seriousness and the measure of gravity of offence cannot

---

1. Allahabad Bank Vs Prem Narain Panda and Others 1996(1) Bank CLR 98 (S.C.)
2. UCO Bank and Others Vs Sushil Kumar Saha A.I.R 2013 S.C (Civil) 362
3. Central Bank of India Vs C. Barnard 1991(1) S.C.C. 319, 1991(1) Bank CLR 311 (S.C.)
4. Probin Kumar Phukan Vs Union of India and Others 2002(2) Bank CLR 753 (Gau)
5. M. Kasi Vs Indian Bank 1994(2) Bank CLR 560 (Madras)

be standardised and punishment would vary on the facts of each case. If an employee of the Bank indulges in fraud, cheating or misappropriation, such acts cannot be viewed lightly but are required to be dealt with severely so that it has a desired effect of non-repetition and discouraging others in indulging in similar activities. While dealing with the delinquency of officers in nationalised banks, the overall national interest must be borne in mind and the impact, misdeeds of officers make on the customers. Such delinquencies need to have a serious view. Once an act of misappropriation is proved, may it be for a small or large amount, there is no question showing uncalled sympathy and consideration of past record and any such consideration of past record is absolutely in the discretion of management in appropriate cases and Court cannot substitute penalty in such cases.[1]

The question of quantum of punishment is within the discretion of the Disciplinary Authority/management. The punishment should suit the guilt and guilty. It should not be vindictive or unduly harsh. It should not be as disproportionate to the offence as to shock the conscience and amount in itself to conclusive evidence of bias.

Often, the Delinquent Officer demands for personal hearing before Disciplinary Authority. If Conduct Regulations provide any hearing before the Disciplinary Authority, it becomes the right of Delinquent Officer. Under departmental inquiry when Inquiring Authority reaches to the conclusion that guilt/misconduct of the charge-sheeted employee has been proved, the question of punishment arises. The punishment is to be awarded on the basis of inquiry report by Disciplinary Authority. A punishment should commensurate with the guilt. It will always be open to Delinquent Officer to plead his case for a mitigating punishment and error of judgment will also be a ground for mitigating the punishment. The Disciplinary Authority cannot overlook the factors pleaded by Delinquent Officer which might contribute to error of judgment on his part which in turn led to commission of misconducts by him. Thus, where the element of intention to defraud the Bank cannot be said to be proved with certainty, punishment should not be deterrent.

Punishment may be of various types as defined is concerned with the Officers' Conduct Regulations. Broadly speaking, they are:

- Dismissal from services of Bank
- Discharge from services of Bank
- Compulsory retirement from the service
- Lowering down the increments
- Stopping of increment/s
- Recovery of loss caused to Bank due to misconduct
- Censure/Reprimand

1. V.R. Kuttapan Vs State Bank of Travancore and Others 2002(1) Bank CLR 256 (Kerala)

**Reversion to lower post:** A direct recruit cannot be reverted to a lower post. It is only a promotee who can be reverted from the promotion post to lower post from which he was promoted. This is the elementary proposition in this type of punishment. However, when an employee has been awarded the punishment of reversion to lower post, the same cannot be a ground for setting aside the entire proceedings because it will be a mere technical plea against the "Decision-making process".

In another matter where the Delinquent Officer agreed to accept reversion to lower post but in writ raised the technical plea that he cannot be reverted to lower post than that to which he was appointed, the High Court refused to entertain the plea and punishment was kept intact.[1]

The question of choice and quantum of punishment is within the jurisdiction and discretion of the department.[2]

An order of dismissal or removal from the service can be passed only when an employee is in service. If a person is not in employment, the question of terminating his service ordinarily would not arise unless there is a specific Regulation in that behalf.[3]

The validity, legality and propriety of the order of Disciplinary Authority is likely to be considered with reference to the grounds raised by the Delinquent Officer in appeal. Therefore, where the Delinquent Officer fails to take any objection in appeal regarding non-consideration of written submission of the Delinquent Officer by the Inquiring Authority, he cannot be allowed to raise the objection in writ petition.[4]

Whether the impugned punishment is so disproportionate as to shock the conscience of the Court, is a question of fact, which has to be decided on the facts of each case, having regard to the gravity of the misconduct, nature of the duties discharged by the Delinquent Officer, the position held by him and the nexus between the official position and the misconduct. It will not be practicable to lay down as to when a punishment can be said to be shocking the judicial conscience. Considering the fact that there is no misappropriation and no loss to Bank due to negligence of the Delinquent Officer, High Court held that imposition of penalty of stoppage of four increments with cumulative effect was disproportionate to the charges leveled and accordingly penalty was reduced to stoppage of two increments without cumulative effect.[5]

Similarly, where the charges were that the Delinquent Officer failed to obtain proper sanction for availing loan for himself and raised loans from outside agencies without apprising controlling authority, the penalty of removal from services was held highly disproportionate to the gravity of charges leveled against him.[6]

---

1. Vipin Kumar Agarwal Vs Board of Director, Vidur Gramin Bank, Bijnor through its Chairman 1990(1) Bank CLR 527 Allahabad
2. Rajendra Pai Vs Canara Bank 1989(1) Bank CLR 127
3. Rajendra Shankar Shukla Vs UCO Bank 2008(1) Bank CLR 610
4. Rakshit N. Majumdar Vs General Manager, Dena Bank and Others 1998(1) Bank CLR 366 (Gujarat)
5. S. Sridhar Vs Tungbhadra Gramin Bank 2000(1) Bank CLR 143 (Kant)
6. C.R. Kodanda Raman Vs The Chief General Manager, State Bank of India, Hyderabad and Another 2000(1) Bank CLR 630 (A.P.)

Looking to the circumstances that admittedly there was no financial loss to the Bank on occurrence of the improprieties committed by the Delinquent Officer and there was no evidence of dishonest concealment or suppression by the Delinquent Officer and the Delinquent Officer had duly reported all the transactions in periodical returns and that no objection was raised in that behalf during the periodical inspections and therefore High Court remitted back the matter to the Bank to consider for lesser punishment.

Where an employee having rendered fifty years service was awarded punishment of dismissal on the charge of misappropriation of ₹ 200 (two hundred) while working as chief cashier, the employee failed to bring into the notice of the authorities the excess amount of cash in his possession, the punishment of dismissal was held disproportionate and too harsh.[1]

Where an Assistant Manager was awarded punishment of removal from services for the charges, i.e., for the temporary overdraft, purchase of cheques while his Branch Manager was awarded with punishment of withholding of one increment; quashing the punishment of Assistant Manager on the ground of being discriminatory reinstatement was made and punishment was reduced to severe warning and 75% of his salary for the period from the date of removal to the date of reinstatement.[2] The above judgment of Allahabad High Court was reversed while holding that High Court did not record as to how and why it found the punishment shockingly disproportionate; even if a co-Delinquent Officer is given lesser punishment it cannot be a ground for interference. Mere expression of High Court that the punishment is shockingly disproportionate would not meet the requirement of law and the matter was remitted back to High Court for fresh considerations by Supreme Court.[3]

When the Delinquent Officer was able to show with the help of another order passed by Disciplinary Authority imposing punishment of reduction of basic pay inclusive of stagnation of increment and FPA on an officer employee against whom similar and more serious charges were established in inquiry, the punishment of removal from service was reduced to penalty of reduction to a lower grade or post or to a lower stage in a time scale leaving it to Competent Authority in Bank to determine the proportion of pay and allowances which should be granted to the Delinquent Officer.[4]

In another matter, Delinquent Officer raised objection that though the Delinquent Officer and the branch manager both were charge-sheeted for misappropriation of amount in collision and both were found guilty, the Branch Manager was permitted to retire while an order of dismissal was imposed on the Delinquent Officer but

---

1. G.C. Tondon S/o Badrinath Tondon Vs Central Bank of India 1992(1) Bank CLR 345 Allahabad
2. P.C. Kakkar Vs Chairman/Managing Director, United Commercial Bank 2001(2) Bank CLR 291 (Allahabad)
3. Chairman and Managing Director, United Commercial Bank and Others Vs P.C. Kakkar 2003(1) Bank CLR 622 (S.C.)
4. Probin Kumar Phukan Vs Union of India and Others 2002(2) Bank CLR 753 (Gau)

dismissal order having been passed after taking into consideration the past record which was not without blemish the order was upheld.[1]

It is not only the amount involved but the mental set-up, the type of duty performed and similar relevant circumstances will be considered in decision-making process.

Yet in another matter where the Delinquent Officer was convicted and sentenced in a criminal case under Sections 420, 120B, 465, 467, 468, 477 I.P.C. read with Section 5(2) of Prevention of Corruption Act and under Disciplinary Action/ Proceedings, punishment of dismissal from Bank services was made, stressing that a punishment should be moderate having regard to the charges proved, the total length of service and past record, and accordingly the punishment was reduced by converting termination order into compulsory retirement.[2]

In a matter Allahabad High Court[3] while settling the quantum of punishment took into account the following:

"*(a) The petitioner had throughout an unblemished service record.*

*(b) Infraction of duty, if any, responsible for loss to the Bank was not of a gravity or of serious/extreme nature which warranted dismissal from service.*

*(c) The appellant can be called upon to mitigate seriousness of lapse on his part and restore the interest of the Bank by depositing the amount in question, in the instant case as observed the Apex Court, about ₹ 46000/- (Rupees Forty Six Thousand only).*

*(d) The petitioner (employee in question) has already attained the age of superannuation on August, 1994 and in that view of the matter he is not going to be reinstated in the service of the Bank so as to give rise to apprehension on the part of the employer of any nature like loss of trust and confidence or recurrence of similar lapse in nature. On the other hand, the minor punishment in the nature of awarding adverse entry like warning and/ or censure entry even if now awarded shall be of no relevance and will serve no purpose because the petitioner has already retired.*

*(e) The employee was subjected to Disciplinary Action/Proceedings in the year 1987 and he has been compelled to enter into litigation up to Apex Court. This petition is part of second inning. Thus, it is evident that petitioner has spent considerable amount on this litigation.*"

**Imposing of multiple penalties:** Imposition of more than one penalty for one charge has been a point of debate. Generally, for one charge, there can be one penalty whether minor or major.

---

1. Dattatray Trimbak Kulkarni Vs State Bank of India, Bombay 1993(1) Bank CLR 704
2. Arun Sood Vs United Commercial Bank and Others 2001(2) Bank CLR 307 (H.P.)
3. Kailash Nath Gupta Vs Enquiry Officer (Sri R.K. Rai), Allahabad Bank Regional Office, Allahabad 2004(1) Bank CLR 172 (Allahabad)

Supreme Court[1] has clarified the position by observing. "*The Disciplinary Authority, therefore, in our opinion acted illegally and without jurisdiction in imposing the both minor and major penalty by the same order. Such a course of action could not have been taken in law.*"

Following above dictum, Chhattisgarh High Court[2] quashed the order where Disciplinary Authority has imposed a penalty of dismissal, i.e., major penalty and minor penalty of reduction of basic pay by two stages and censure.

Kerala High Court has taken the view that even if misconduct is proved, the Disciplinary Authority cannot impose two penalties. Accordingly, a penalty of censure and recovery from the pay of the Delinquent Officer was quashed.[3] However, Rajasthan High Court took a different view[4] in the circumstances when Disciplinary Authority passed an order of punishment as under—

"*Charge No. 1. Proved — Reduction of basic pay of Shri Gupta to the lowest basic pay in time scale (JMG I) applicable to him*

*Charge No. 2. Proved — Censure*

*Charge No. 3. Proved — Censure*

*Charge No. 4. Proved — Recovery of ₹ 75,000/- from pay and allowances or terminal banefits of Shri Gupta or such other amount as may be due to him*

*Charge No. 5. Proved — Withholding promotion for a period of five years from the date of this order*

*Charge No. 7. Proved — Censure*

*Charge No. 8. Proved — Reduction of basic pay of Shri Gupta to the lowest basic pay in the lowest time scale (JMG I) applicable to him*

*The above penalties are to run concurrently.*"

Interpreting Regulation 7(3), the High Court held that though in concluding part of the Regulation the word 'penalty' has been used in contrast to word 'penalties' in first part yet it cannot be said that multiple penalties cannot be passed but word 'any' will be interpreted as word 'all' in the context of Regulations and accordingly multiple penalties as above were upheld.

## 1. ROLE OF VIGILANCE DEPARTMENT

Vigilance cases are monitored by the Government/Central Vigilance Commission/ Reserve Bank of India and there is continuous assessment of the performance of each Bank in the field of pending inquiries. In view of Government Directives, each Bank avoids to bring any inquiry into the bracket of old inquiry. Chief Vigilance

1. Union of India and Another Vs S.C. Parashar 2006(109) F.L.R. 228 (S.C.) 2006(40) A.I.R. 701 (S.C.), 2006(3) S.C.C. 167
2. Rajendra Shankar Shukla Vs UCO Bank 2008(1) Bank CLR 610 (Chhattisgarh)
3. Abdul Kareem Vs Canara Bank 1997(2) Bank CLR 235 (Kerala)
4. Shri Satya Narain Gupta Vs UCO Bank and Others 2004(2) Bank CLR 685 Rajasthan

Commissioner and Vigilance Department of Bank though constitute a monitoring agency but their say off the record is natural.

There is empowerment of Bank to consult the Central Vigilance Commission, whenever necessary in respect of all disciplinary cases having vigilance angle.

There can be no precise limits but generally following types of cases are treated as having vigilance angle —

- Taking or demanding bribe or receiving gratification.
- Fraud or attempted fraud.
- Tempering with or destruction of any record.
- Exercising authority in his favour or in favour of close kin with a view to deriving advantage.
- Breach of faith in performance of his duty.
- Deriving pecuniary benefit or any other advantage for himself or for anybody else through misrepresentation or suppression of material facts.
- Drawing unjustified or unwarranted allowance or remuneration or benefit without authority/sanction or obtaining such sanction by misrepresentation of facts.
- Gross irregularities or negligence in the discharge of official duties with dishonest motives.
- Misuse of official position or powers for personal gain.
- Disclosure of secret or confidential information.
- False claim like TA Bills, Medical bills etc.
- Allegations referring to any act involving lack of integrity or of bribery or of corruption.

In cases involving vigilance angle, the Disciplinary Authority consults Vigilance Department of Bank about the proposed punishment. The common question arises whether any extraneous matter not on record of inquiry has effected the decision. Generally, Disciplinary Authority prepares a tentative punishment order and the same is sent to Vigilance Department for approval. But since such tentative order is not served upon the Delinquent Officer employee, therefore, it does not take finality. The Vigilance Department expresses its views over the tentative order and may express the view that Delinquent Officer deserves a more severe punishment and may request to re-examine the proposed punishment. After considering such view., Disciplinary Authority passes final order. But Vigilance Department neither can issue any direction to impose a higher punishment nor can alter the finding regarding guilt. It can merely give its opinion that gravity of proved charge did warrant a higher penalty to the Delinquent Officer.

The advice tendered by Chief Vigilance Commissioner/Chief Vigilance Officer is not binding on the punishing authority and it is not obligatory upon the punishing authority to accept the advice of Chief Vigilance Commissioner. No third party like Chief Vigilance Commissioner or Central Government could dictate Disciplinary Authority or the Appellate Authority as to how they should exercise their power and what punishment they should impose on the Delinquent Officer[1] where Chief Vigilance Commissioner recommended behind the back of Delinquent Officer and arrived at its own findings relating to guilt contrary to the findings of Inquiring Authority and such findings were accepted by Disciplinary Authority without giving any opportunity of hearing to the Delinquent Officer to comment upon the order of Disciplinary Authority was held to be vitiated.[2]

Again where Chief Vigilance Commissioner's report formed part of the report of inquiry and was taken into consideration by Disciplinary Authority but the same was not supplied to the Delinquent Officer employee, it was held that the omission has vitiated the order of dismissal.[3]

Summing up, so long as the decision is not on the dictates of the Vigilance Department or other outside authority but on independent consideration, the punishment order cannot be faulted. It cannot be said that either the act of intimating the Vigilance Department about the inquiry or independently reconsidering the issue of penalty after receiving the view of Vigilance Department amounted to be acting on extraneous material or activity on the advice or recommendation or direction of the Chief Vigilance Officer.[4]

Where Vigilance Commission advised removal of both the Delinquent Officers (AFO and Branch Manager) but Disciplinary Authority awarded the punishment of withholding of two increments in relation to Branch Manager by observing that it is a case of mere irregularity and order of removal of the other, Delinquent Officer was passed by observing that it is a case of misappropriation. The application of mind by Disciplinary Authority is apparent because Disciplinary Authority has not followed the advice of Vigilance Department blindly and therefore no discrimination in awarding punishment can be said.[5]

## 2. ROLE OF APPELLATE AUTHORITY

The Appellate Authority in the inquiring department is final authority on facts. Therefore, it should appreciate the evidence produced before Inquiring Authority/ Primary Authority merely because it is an Appellate Authority. It cannot brush aside the reasoning or findings recorded but the Primary Authority. It is not necessary to reappraise evidence to arrive at the same findings.[6]

---

1. Nagraj Shivrao Karjagi Vs Syndicate Bank 1991(3) S.C.C. 219
2. State Bank of India Vs D.C. Agrawal 1993(1) S.C.C. 13, 1992(2) Bank CLR 596 (S.C.)
3. Mohammad Quaranuddin (dead) by LRs Vs State of Andhra Pradesh 1994(5) S.C.C. 118
4. State Bank of India and Others Vs S.N. Goyal 2009(1) Bank CLR 591 (S.C.)
5. S. Narsimha Reddy Vs Personnel Manager, Syndicate Bank Manipal and Others 1993(2) Bank CLR 685 (A.P.)
6. State Bank of Bikaner and Jaipur Vs Prabhu Dayal Grover, Judgment Today, 1995(7) S.C. 207; A.I.R. 1995 S.C. 320

Disciplinary authority and on appeal Appellate Authority being fact-finding authorities have exclusive power to consider the evidence with a view to maintain discipline. They are invested with the discretion to impose appropriate punishment keeping in view the magnitude or gravity of the misconduct. If the punishment imposed by the Disciplinary Authority or Appellate Authority shocks the conscience of the Court, then only the Court may interfere with the punishment awarded to Delinquent Officer.[1]

*The power of the Appellate Authority is always unlimited and on being satisfied it can substitute its decision for the order which is appealed against.*

Where Disciplinary Authority has recorded findings on each one of the charges on the basis of the findings recorded by the Inquiring Authority and sufficient reasons are contained in the order of the Inquiring Authority, it will not be necessary for Appellate Authority to delve itself into the matter in detail and to provide detailed reasons, if such reasons are available in the original order.

Thus, while disposing an appeal, a single line communication was sent to the Delinquent Officer that his services are terminated, it was held that internal note/memorandum to the Board was having full facts therefore there was no need to communicate the detailed reasons.[2] But it does not mean that Appellate Authority should consider nothing. An Appellate Authority has to apply its mind in general on the following points—

(i) Whether procedure of inquiry has been as per the Conduct Regulations of the Bank and if not what prejudice has been caused to the Delinquent Officer.

(ii) Whether the findings of Disciplinary Authority are warranted by the evidence on record under inquiry.

(iii) Whether the penalty imposed is adequate and commensurate with the guilt.

Finally, the orders of Appellate Authority cannot be passed in a mechanical manner. Appellate Authority has authority to go into the question of facts as also question of law. It is open to it to consider the legality and propriety of the order passed by the Disciplinary Authority. The Appellate Authority is expected to apply its mind to representations which an appellant make in the grounds of appeal. Where Appellate Authority was found to have passed many orders in identical terms without application of mind to the facts of the case and without disclosing the reasoning of Appellate Authority, the orders were quashed.[3]

Summing up, though an Appellate Authority is not expected to write a detailed judgment, it is at least to record its reason even if brief so that it can be gathered it

---

1. Ram Autar Garg (since deceased) through his LRs Vs General Manager (Personnel Division), Punjab National Bank, New Delhi and Others 2000(2) Bank CLR 88 (All)
2. Indian Overseas Bank (Represented by its General Manager) Madras Vs R. Sathyamoorthy 1994(1) Bank CLR 394
3. Sada Shiva Pandey Vs State Bank of India and Others 1994(1) Bank CLR 626

had considered the relevant aspects of the matter before reaching its conclusion. Particularly when Appellate Authority reverses the order or Disciplinary Authority should give sufficient reasons for reversing the earlier order.

## 3. PERSONAL HEARING BEFORE APPELLATE AUTHORITY

Under Conduct Regulations of Bank, generally an Appellate Authority is not required to give any personal hearing to the Delinquent Officer even where it proposes to enhance the punishment. But in case of enhancement of punishment, a show cause notice is required to be given whereafter Appellate Authority may pass final orders after taking into account the representation if any submitted by the Delinquent Officer. But even in that case, the provision of personal hearing is not generally available in Conduct Regulations of Bank. Further, though a Delinquent Officer might have asked for personal hearing and the same might have been refused but under judicial review, Delinquent Officer has to establish that prejudice has been caused to him due to non-affording of personal hearing.

Where in reply to the show cause memo for enhancement of punishment, the Delinquent Officer submitted his objections but Reviewing Authority did not clearly give the reasons in dealing with the objections of the Delinquent Officer, the order enhancing the punishment was quashed.[1]

Regulation providing powers of review can be applied when Disciplinary Action/ Proceedings has not attained finality.

So far as *review* is concerned, Conduct Regulations specifically provides for the same. In a case where admittedly the two charge-sheets were issued and in one of them the Delinquent Officer was exonerated and the second charge-sheet was not followed up despite submission of Inquiry Report but Reviewing Authority in purported exercise of his powers under concerned Regulation (Regulation 18 of Conduct Regulations) passed an order setting aside the findings of Inquiring Authority after six years of the exoneration of the Delinquent Officer. In the case an appeal of Bank, Supreme Court[2] clarified that the powers for exercising review were not exercised within a reasonable time and accordingly appeal of bank was dismised.

Summing up, every authority under Conduct Regulations should know that Regulations have statutory force. An authority exercising such statutory powers is required to act within the four corners thereof. Authority is bound by the limitations prescribed under Conduct Regulations. Therefore, the Disciplinary Proceedings require their disposal with caution and care.

1. Jitendra Pal Singh Bhadauria Vs Chairman and Managing Director and Reviewing Authority, Allahabad Bank 1998(1) Bank CLR 463 (All)
2. Canara Bank and Others Vs Swapan Kumar Pant and Others 2006(2) Bank CLR 44 (S.C.)

# CHAPTER 10

# JUDICIAL REVIEW OF INQUIRY

1. **Proportionality of Punishment**
2. **Territorial Jurisdiction of High Court**

It is natural that in number of cases an approach is made to Courts by Delinquent Officer challenging the conduction and decision of Disciplinary Action/Proceedings. This is done generally by way of filing a writ petition before concerned High Court.

The scope in *writ jurisdiction* is very limited one for reviewing an inquiry yet it is obligatory on the part of Court to ensure that Disciplinary Action/Proceedings are held in accordance with rules and principles of natural justice. The jurisdiction of Court to interfere with the disciplinary matters of punishment cannot be equated with an appellate jurisdiction. The Court cannot interfere with the findings of Inquiring Authority or of Competent Authority where they are not arbitrary or utterly perverse. A perverse finding is one which is based on no evidence or one that no reasonable person would arrive at. Perverse finding is not only against the weight of evidence but is altogether against the evidence itself. Dictionary meaning of word 'perverse' is as turned wrong way, not right, distorted from the right, turned away or deviation from what is right, proper and correct. Courts are always drawing distinction line between the decisions which are perverse and those which are not. If a decision is arrived at on no evidence or evidence which is thoroughly unreliable and no reasonable person would act upon it, the order would be perverse. But if there is some evidence on record which is acceptable and which could be relied upon, howsoever compendious, it may be the conclusions would not be treated as perverse.

If there has been an inquiry consistent with the rules of the Bank and in accordance with the principles of natural justice, what punishment would meet the end of justice is a matter exclusively within the jurisdiction of the Competent Authority. The adequacy of penalty, unless it is malafide, is certainly not a matter for the Court/ Tribunal to concern with.

In exercise of jurisdiction under Article 226 of the Constitution of India, the power of the High Court while considering the question of *proportionality of punishment in service matters,* is one of judicial review which is not an appeal from a decision but a review of the manner in which the decision was made. If the punishment awarded by the Disciplinary Authority is one, which having regard to the rules, could be imposed for the proved misconduct, the Court will not go into the sufficiency or otherwise of the punishment awarded by the authority. Interference with the punishmen imposed by the authorities after finding the Delinquent Officer/Official guilty in a Disciplinary Action/Proceedings is strictly speaking not within the jurisdiction of the Courts within normal course. But then it should also be borne in mind that there are cases and that it is not possible to lay down any pre-determined principle which may be applicable to all the cases and in all the situations. The essence of the matter is for the Court to take into consideration all relevant factors and to balance and weigh them to determine whether the punishment imposed is commensurate with the gravity of misconduct. *Where the punishment is overtly excessive, the principles laid down in the various decisions which are applicable in all normal cases would become inapplicable.* Supreme Court[1] relying upon Wednessbury principle laid down that interference with punishment is not permissible unless one or the other conditions are satisfied, namely, the order was contrary to law or relevant factors were not considered or irrelevant factors were considered or the decision was one which no reasonable person could have taken. Where undisputedly past track record is unsatisfactory inasmuch the Delinquent Officer was found guilty at earlier three occasions, punishment of compulsory retirement was not disturbed.[2] The limitations and parameters under Article 226 of the Constitution of India in regard to interference with punishment were summarised by Calcutta High Court[3] as under:

1. whether the Appellate Authority has applied its mind or not
2. whether the charges in its *prima facie* value constitute misconduct
3. whether Inquiry Report is based on evidence or in consonance with the principle of natural justice
4. whether order of punishment is based on law findings of guilt.

---

1. Chairman and Managing Director, United Commercial Bank and Others Vs P.C. Kakkar 2003(1) Bank CLR 622 (S.C.)
2. Govardhan Singh Vs Syndicate Bank and Another 2004(2) Bank CLR 695 (Rajasthan)
3. Venkatarama Murlidhar Shenoy Vs Syndicate Bank 2001(2) Bank CLR 48 (Calcutta)

Supreme Court[1] has held in relation to judicial review of departmental action "*.....an order passed imposing a punishment on an employee consequent upon a disciplinary/departmental inquiry in violation of the rules/regulations/statutory provisions governing such inquiries should not be set aside automatically. The Court or the Tribunal should inquire whether (a) the provision violated is of a substantive nature or (b) whether it is procedural in character.*

(1) A substantive provision has normally to be complied with and the theory of substantial compliance or the test of prejudice would not be applicable in such a case.

(2) In a case of violation of a procedural provision, the position is this: procedural provisions are generally meant for affording a reasonable and adequate opportunity to the Delinquent Officer/employee. They are, generally speaking, conceived in his interest. Violation of any and every procedural provision cannot be said to automatically vitiate the inquiry held or order passed. Except cases falling under 'no notice', 'no opportunity' and 'no hearing' categories, the question will be whether procedural violation has prejudiced the Delinquent Officer/employee in defending himself properly and effectively. If it is found that he has been prejudice, appropriate orders have to be made to repair and remedy the prejudice including the setting aside of the enquiry and/or the order of punishment.

If no prejudice is established to have resulted therefrom, the inquiry will be good. There may be certain procedural provisions which are of a fundamental character, whose violation is by itself proof of prejudice. The Court may not insist on proof of prejudice in such cases. For example, we may take a case where there is a provision expressly providing that after the evidence of the employee/government is over, the employee shall be given an opportunity to lead defense in his evidence, and in a given case, the Inquiring Authority does not give that opportunity in spite of the Delinquent Officer/employee asking for it. The prejudice is self-evident. No proof of prejudice as such need be called for in such a case. To repeat, the test is one of prejudice, i.e., whether the person has received a fair hearing considering all things. Now, this very aspect can also be looked at from the point of view of directory and mandatory provisions if one is so inclined. Principle stated under 4(a) herein below is only other way of looking at the same aspect as is dealt with herein and not a distinct or different principle.

(3) (a) In the case of a procedural provision which is not of a mandatory character, the complaint of violation will be examined from the standpoint of substantial compliance. Be that as it may, the order passed in violation of such a provision can be set aside only where such violation has occasioned prejudice to the Delinquent Officer/employee.

1. State Bank of Patiala Vs S.K. Sharma 1996(II), Labour Law Judgment 296, 1996(2) Bank CLR 59 (S.C.), 1996 Bankers' Journal 447 (S.C.), Judgment Today 1996(3) (S.C.) 722

(b) In the case of violation of a procedural provision, which is of a mandatory character, it has to be ascertained whether the provision is conceived in the interest of the person proceeded against or in public interest. If it is found to be the former, then it must be seen whether the Delinquent Officer has waived the said requirement, either expressly or by his conduct. If he is found to have waived it, then the order of punishment cannot be set aside on the ground of said violation. If, on the other hand, it is found that the Delinquent Officer/employee has not waived it or that the provision could not be waived by him, then the Court or Tribunal will make appropriate directions (include the setting aside of the order of punishment). Keeping in mind the approach adopted by the Constitution Bench in B. Karunakar, 1994 AIR SCW 1050, the ultimate test is always the same, viz., test of prejudice or the test of fair hearing, as it may be called.

(4) Where the inquiry is not governed by any rules/regulations/statutory provisions and the only obligation is to observe the principles of natural justice—or, for that matter, wherever such principles are held to be implied by the very nature and impact of the order/action, the Court or the Tribunal should make a distinction between a total violation of natural justice (rule of *audi alteram partem*) and violation of a facet of the said rule. In other words, a distinction must be made between 'no opportunity' and 'no adequate opportunity', i.e., between 'no notice', 'no hearing' and 'no fair hearing'.

(a) In the case of former, the order passed would undoubtedly be invalid. In such cases, normally, liberty will be reserved for the Authority to take proceedings afresh according to law, i.e., in accordance with the said rule (*audi alteram partem*).

(b) But in the later case, the effect of violation of a facet of the rule (*audi alteram partem*) has to be examined from the standpoint of prejudice. In other words, what the Court or Tribunal has to see is whether in the totality of the circumstances, the Delinquent Officer/employee did or did not have a fair hearing and the orders to be made shall depend upon the answer to the said query. (It is made clear that this principle does not apply in the case of rule against bias, the test in which behalf are laid down elsewhere).

(5) While applying the rule of *audi alteram partem* (the primary principle of natural justice), the Court/Tribunal/Authority must always bear in mind the ultimate and overriding objective underlying the said rule, viz., to ensure a fair hearing and to ensure that there is no failure of justice. It is this objective which should guide them in applying the rule to varying situations that arise before them.

(6) There may be situations where the interests of State or public interest may call for a curtailing or the rule of *audi alteram partem*. In such situations,

the Court may have to balance public/State interest with the requirement of natural justice and arrive at an appropriate decision."

## 1. PROPORTIONALITY OF PUNISHMENT

In cases where Court is unsatisfied with the quantum of punishment, normal course will be to remit the matter to management for a fresh decision as to the quantum of punishment. Only in rare cases where there has been long delay in the time taken by Disciplinary Action/Proceedings and in the time taken in the Courts and in such extreme or rare cases, Court can substitute its own view as to the quantum of punishment.[1] Accordingly, Karnataka High Court[2] finding the punishment of compulsory retirement successive, the same was mitigated to punishment of reduction to the next lower grade with continuity of service and 25% of back wages. In another matter where the dismissal was made for unauthorised absence maintaining the punishment, High Court directed the Bank to pay a lump-sum to the Delinquent Officer.[3]

Whether the proved misconduct is a substantial misconduct or a trivial misconduct, is a matter which can be examined by the High Court; and where the Disciplinary Authority proceeded on the assumption that the misconduct was a substantial misconduct whereas in fact it was found to be only a trivial misconduct, the High Court will be well within its bounds to quash the impugned punishment as one not authorised by law.

Where single judge passed an order as follows:

*"...the Disciplinary Authority and the Appellate Authority ought to have approached the matter with compassion and any person who has committed an offence of this nature and who has realised his mistake and seeks an opportunity to reform himself should have been given an opportunity and it is only in that context the Disciplinary Authority and Appellate Authority should have approached the question of imposition of punishment."* But in appeal Division Bench of Delhi High Court[4] reversed the order and held *"in banking business, absolute devotion, diligence, integrity and honesty have to be preserved by the bank employees otherwise confidence of the public and the depositors would be shaken...."*

Judicial review confines itself with the decision-making process and not the decision. It is for the Disciplinary Authority to consider what would be nature of punishment to be imposed on the Delinquent Officer. The Court while dealing with the quantum of punishment is to record reasons as to why it is felt that punishment was not commensurate with the proved charges. Therefore, interference is limited

---

1. Delhi Development Authority Vs Skippers Constructions Co. (Pvt.) Ltd. and Another 2003(1) Bank CLR 203 (S.C.)
2. M.C. Charati Vs Personnel Manager and Disciplinary Authority, Syndicate Bank 2001(2) Bank CLR 90 (Kant)
3. Y.P. Sarabhai Vs Union Bank of India and Another 2006(2) Bank CLR 677 (S.C.)
4. Syndicate Bank Vs Bakhtawar Singh 2001(2) Bank CLR 415 (Delhi)

and restricted to only exceptional cases. When there are no allegations of procedural irregularities/illegality and there is no violation of principles of natural justice, the bald allegations of malafides will not be acceptable.[1]

While making review of punishment and appraising proportionality of punishment, it is clear that principles under Section 11-A of Industrial Dispute Act cannot be engrafted into the Disciplinary Action/Proceedings either in relation to Government servant or other employee whose service conditions are governed by set of rules and not by the Industrial Dispute Act and therefore it will not be open to High Court to reappreciate the material on the basis of which Inquiring Authority arrives at its conclusions and came to a different conclusion in second appeal arising out of a suit seeking a declaration that dismissal order is illegal.

## 2. TERRITORIAL JURISDICTION OF HIGH COURT

The place of filing of petition is either the place where the order is passed or the place where it is communicated, which would determine and govern the territorial jurisdiction.[2]

Where order of punishment passed by Disciplinary Authority is sustained by Appellate Authority and by Reviewing Authority and both, such Authorities are outside the territorial jurisdiction and the records of Disciplinary Action/Proceedings and appellate and review proceedings are also lying outside the territorial jurisdiction of Court, merely because a review application was sent from the place of High Court and is transferred within the territory of High Court, will not constitute any part of cause of action arising within the territorial jurisdiction and communication of the order of review will be of no consequence.[3]

So far as *remedy in Civil Court* is concerned, the relationship of master and servant is purely contractual, and it is well settled that a contract of personal service is not specifically enforceable, having regard to the bar contained in Section 14 of the Specific Relief Act, 1963. Even if the termination of the contract of employment (by dismissal or otherwise) is found to be illegal or in breach, the remedy of the employee is only to seek damages and not specific performance. Courts will neither declare such termination to be a nullity nor declare that the contract of employment subsists nor grant the consequential relief of reinstatement. The three well-recognised exceptions to this rule are:[4]

(i) where a civil servant is removed from service in contravention of the provision of Article 311 of the Constitution of India (or any law made under Article 309);

1. Bank of India Vs T. Jogram 2008(1) Bank CLR 161 (S.C.)
2. Bhanu Prasad Vs State Bank of Bikaner and Jaipur and Others 1990(1) Bank CLR 84 (H.C. M.P. Indore Bench).
3. Chowdhury Niranjan Mahapatra Vs Andhra Bank and Others 1990(2) Bank CLR 193
4. Vaish Degree College and Others Vs Laxmi Narain and Others A.I.R. 1976 S.C. 888

(ii) where a workman having protection of Industrial Disputes Act, 1947 is wrongly terminated from service; and

(iii) where an employee of a statutory body is terminated from service in breach or violation of any mandatory provision of a statute or statutory rules.

There is, thus, clear distinction between public employment governed by statutory rules and private employment governed purely by contract. The test for deciding the nature of relief – damages or reinstatement with consequential reliefs – is whether the employment is governed purely by contract or by a statute or statutory rules.

Even where the employer is a statutory body, where the relationship is purely governed by contract with no element of statutory governance, the contract of personal service will not be specifically enforceable. Conversely, where the employer is a non-statutory body, but the employment is governed by a statute or statutory rules, a declaration that the termination is null and void and the employee should be reinstated can be granted by Courts.

A Cooperative Bank where State Government exercise all-pervasive control over the bank and its employees and the service conditions of such employees are governed by statutory rules prescribing entire gamut of procedure of initiation of Disciplinary Action/Proceedings by framing a set of charges and culminating in inflicting of appropriate punishment after complying with the requirements of giving a show cause, the conclusion will be irrespective that Bank is an instrumentality of State and therefore when Bank did not follow mandatory provisions of the rules and regulations and passed the order of termination in gross violation of 'natural justice', the third exception to the general principle that contract of personal service cannot specifically be enforced will apply and accordingly the Delinquent Officer was reinstated in service.[1]

In the matters of officers of private banks, the High Court cannot issue writ because such private banks are not stated within the meaning of Article 12 of Constitution of India. In case of private banks, no financial assistance is extended either by Government or by State Government or by Reserve Bank of India and Private Banks cannot be said to be enjoying any monopoly status conferred by Government. Merely control under Banking Regulation Act, 1949 does not amount to pervasive State control.

1. Ram Sahan Rai Vs Sachiv Samanya Prabandhak and Another 2001(1) Bank CLR 523 (S.C.)

# CHAPTER 11

# SUSPENSION AND REINSTATEMENT

1. **Subsistence Allowance**
2. **Payment of Wages Related to Suspension Period after Rejoining of Duties**
3. **Consequences of Reinstatement**

The meaning of word 'suspension' is 'to attempt', 'to cause' to cease for a time or 'to discontinue temporarily'. Any contract between master and servant involves material obligations which requires each party to perform its part of contract. A contract can, however, be kept in abeyance and suspended temporarily. During the period of suspension, the contracting parties are absolve of all or some of their obligations.

Law is well settled that an officer employee can be placed under suspension in contemplation of a Disciplinary Action/Proceedings or with the initiation of a Disciplinary Action/Proceedings against him or if any criminal cases pending/ registered etc.

Suspension is not a punishment and it is made both in the interest of the employee as well as employer so that both may be made free to concentrate upon establishing the truth. Because of order of suspension, the employee does not cease to be a member as it is an administrative order, not a quasi-judicial order.

Presumption is that the order of suspension is a cessation of jural relationship of master and servant. By keeping the employee under suspension, the relationship of master and servant is not snapped. Instead relationship of master and servant remains in abeyance for a temporary phase. It is an action in order to maintain purity of service when an employee awaiting the result of an inquiry in regard to his suspected misconduct, suspension pending inquiry or in contemplation of Disciplinary Action/ Proceedings does not amount to temporarily removal from service. It is not dependent on the inquiry or/on the charge and/or on the result following from the inquiry because its purpose is to keep an officer out of the sphere of action.

Whenever allegations of misconduct are made, the employee can be suspended. The words 'pending enquiry' in suspension order cannot be construed as pending actual inquiry and it will include outcome of Preliminary Investigation as well.

Suspension is an order for forbidding or disabling the employee to discharge duties of the office or the post held by him. An order of suspension has the effect of debarring the Delinquent Officer from exercising the powers and discharging the duties of his office for the period the same remains in force. The suspended employee retains a lien on the permanent post held by him substantively at the time of suspension and does not suffer a reduction in rank. Further, a suspension order may cause a lasting damage to the Delinquent Officer's reputation even if he is exonerated or found guilty of only a minor misconduct. Therefore, suspension must be a step in aid to the ultimate result of the investigation or inquiry. It should not be a routine order or automatic order. The discretion vested in the Competent Authority in this regard should be exercised with care and caution after taking all factors into its account. Management should take into account the gravity of misconduct sought to be inquired into as well as the evidence before it and it is only after application of mind a suspension order should be passed. But an order of suspension cannot be invalidated only on the ground that at a later stage a minor penalty was imposed.

An employee may also be suspended by the Competent Authority in cases where Appellate/Reviewing Court while setting aside an order imposing the penalty of dismissal, removal, discharge or compulsory retirement directs that a fresh inquiry should be held from the start or from a particular stage. Though there may not be any specific directions regarding suspension itself in the order of the Appellate/Reviewing Authority or Court.

While considering the suspension of an officer in Bank, the following should be considered generally —

(i) Impact of the Delinquent Officer's continuance in Institution while facing Disciplinary Action/Proceedings. In other words, what is in public interest.

(ii) It should not be actuated by malafide arbitrariness or with any ulterior motive.

(iii) Possibility of tempering with documents and witnesses. Merely because a Delinquent Officer is transferred to another branch will not rule out the possibility of tempering with evidence in any manner.

(iv) If the charges are grave enough, the Delinquent Officer should not be allowed to function anywhere before the matter has been finally set at rest after a proper scrutiny or Disciplinary Action/Proceedings.

An employee can be placed under suspension only by a specific order made in writing duly signed by the competent authority. An employee cannot be placed under suspension by verbal order except in cases where suspension takes place automatically with the happening of an event as may be prescribed in Conduct/Service Regulations.

It is settled view that the order of suspension though served on a later date it takes effect from the date of passing of the suspension order.[1]

Though suspension order may have mistakes of trivial nature like wrong name of branch etc., still it will not affect the validity of suspension order.[2]

An officiating Regional Manager is competent enough to pass an order of suspension. An officiating Regional Manager for all practical purposes is the Regional Manager and Conduct Regulations of Bank are to be construed reasonably for the proposition when an officiating Regional Manager exercising all the powers of Regional Manager during the period of his incumbency is deemed to be authorised to act as Competent Authority as provided in Conduct Regulations.[3] A suspension order if passed by an incompetent authority to do so may result—

(i) Setting aside of the order of suspension and;

(ii) Claim for full pay and allowances for the period the employee remained away from the duty due to the order of suspension.

An employee can prefer an appeal against the order of suspension and therefore alternate remedy being available a writ before High Court will not lie.[4]

However, if an incompetent authority passes suspension order, Court is competent to refer the matter to the Competent Authority for a fresh look.[5]

Where preliminary investigation report is submitted pointing out the lapses of the Delinquent Officer and contributing losses to the Bank, the suspension order was upheld.[6]

A writ apprehending placement of the Delinquent Officer under suspension will be premature.[7] So far as revocation of suspension is concerned, it depends upon the

1. P.S. Balasubramanian Vs The Chief General Manager, State Bank of India 1991(1) Bank CLR 233
2. The Canara Bank and Another Vs Mrs. S. Vasundhara 1997(2) Bank CLR 581
3. Dinesh Kumar Agrawal Vs Bank of India 1996(1) Bank CLR 466 (M.P.)
4. K.N. Khandelwal Vs Senior Regional Manager, Punjab National Bank, Kanpur 2000(1) Bank CLR 39 (Allahbad)
5. P. Bucchi Reddy Vs The Warangal District Co-operative Central Bank Ltd. and Others 1996(1) Bank CLR 493 (A.P.)
6. Hem Kanta Saikia and Another Vs United Bank of India 2005(2) Bank CLR 314 (Gau)
7. Debashish Kumar Dutta Vs United Bank of India 2005(2) Bank CLR 608 (Gau)

facts of each case. Where two employees were suspended due to pendency of criminal case, the suspension of one employee out of two was revoked. The other remaining employee also sought revocation of suspension but looking to the gravity of his involvement which was greater, management kept silence over the request. High Court clarified that revocation of suspension is purely an administrative decision with which Court do not interfere.[1]

The ultimate decision rests on the management which should decide as to whether it is necessary to keep a person under suspension.

Prolonged continuance of suspension order does not serve any purpose unless the same is highly necessary. Periodical review at certain intervals may be carried out by the management in order to evaluate the need for continuance of the suspension order.

A long suspension in itself amounts to imposition of punishment without proof of any guilt. The expectation of rule of reasonability is that the Bank as employer should not keep its employee under suspension for unduly long period and indefinitely. Accordingly, continuance of suspension for eight years due to pendency of criminal proceedings will itself justify an order of revocation.[2]

## 1. SUBSISTENCE ALLOWANCE

During the period of suspension, the Delinquent Officer is paid a sum generally called 'suitable allowance or subsistence allowance' and normally it is less than salary; while the Delinquent Officer's salary and other privileges remain in abeyance.

Subsistence Allowance is to be paid in accordance with Service Regulations.

When an employee is suspended, it is obvious that pay and allowances normally admissible to him are not paid. For his survival as well as for the survival of his family members, he is paid subsistence allowance under the service rules. This subsistence allowance is meant for the subsistence of the said employee as well as that of his family members. It is required to be paid to the employee every month, so that he can keep his dependents' body and souls together. It is not a profit or a gift which is paid/given to him. This amount is given to him to meet his bare necessities of life.

It is not on account of any service rendered to the employer that the subsistence is given. Subsistence allowance is not given by way of wages but only with a view to see that the employee struggles to survive in order to face the inquiry. Management is entitled to keep a Delinquent Officer under suspension during the pendency of Disciplinary Action/Proceedings subject to paying him subsistence allowance. However, if there is no express terms/provisions in service regulations, the Delinquent Officer will be entitled for his full remuneration.

---

1. Rampal Singh Vs Regional Manager, Punjab National Bank Regional Office, Moradabad and Others 1999(2) Bank CLR 431 (Allahabad)
2. Dinesh Kumar Agrawal Vs Bank of India 1996(1) Bank CLR 466 (M.P.)

Subsistence allowance will be paid on the basis of basic pay as revised from time to time.[1]

Though the provisions of Section 60, CPC are not applicable but the general principle laid down therein will be applicable. Subsistence allowance is allowance which is meant for the subsistence of the suspended employee and his family member. This amount of subsistence allowance will not be liable to attachment in execution of the decree/award.[2] However, Karnataka High Court partially agreed that immunity under Section 60 of CPC is not available to the suspended employee held that since subsistence allowance is being given equal to salary itself to call, subsistence allowance will be a misnomer and it will be liable for attachment under decree of Court.[3]

## 2. PAYMENT OF WAGES RELATED TO SUSPENSION PERIOD AFTER REJOINING OF DUTIES

On conclusion of inquiry or on reinstatement or on joining the duties either Disciplinary Authority must take care about the wages of suspension period while passing final orders on the inquiry or the Competent Authority has to take a decision as to how the period of suspension is to be treated. While imposing penalty/ exonerating the Delinquent Officer how the suspension period is to be treated as off duty/on duty and whether the employee shall be entitled for any salary/allowances and other benefits which he would have been entitled had he been on duty. The order dealing with payments of suspension period does not require separate notice as per Conduct Regulations because such an order passed by the Disciplinary Authority is a consequential order, provided such order is passed at the conclusion of inquiry since opportunity of hearing already stands in inquiry, the requirement of Principles of Natural Justice stands satisfied in such matters.

Whether subsistence allowance payable to an employee is liable to be adjusted against his pay or allowances if at all he is held to be entitled to them by the Competent Authority. The Competent Authority while deciding whether an employee who is suspended in the circumstances is entitled to his pay and allowances or not and to what extent, if any and whether the period is to be treated as on duty or on leave has to take into consideration in circumstances of each case. It is only such employee who is exonerated/acquitted of all blames/charges and is treated by the Competent Authority as being on duty during the period of suspension that such employee will be entitled for full pay and allowances for the period. An employee suspended due to criminal case but acquitted there is nothing for management to prevent it for conducting an inquiry.[4]

---

1. Dinesh Kumar Agrawal Vs Bank of India 1996(1) Bank CLR 466 (M.P.)
2. Gursharan Singh Ghai Vs The Amritsar Co-operative Bank Ltd., Amritsar and Others 1996(2) Bank CLR 387 (P & H)
3. A.B. Norkady Vs United Bank of India, Bangalore and Others 1995(2) Bank CLR 171 (Kant.)
4. Bishan Chand Gupta Vs Chairman Canara Bank and Others 2006(1) Bank CLR 211 (All)

In other words, Regulations vest the power exclusively with the Bank. This power vested in Bank is *an exception to the general rule of 'no work no pay'* and certainly inequitable to those who have to work and earn their pay, therefore exercising this power is absolutely discretionary for Bank.

Where an employee under suspension pending Disciplinary Action/Proceedings retires normally, he will be paid all arrears of salary/retrial benefits unless there is provision in Service Regulations to continue such inquiry and secondly management exercises such powers to continue Disciplinary Action/Proceedings after retirement. However, in that case even PF, gratuity or retrial benefits cannot be withheld without orders of Competent Authority in this regard. In a case where Service Regulations were not providing any authority to continue Disciplinary Action/Proceedings, it was presumed that inquiry has lapsed and the Delinquent Officer was found entitled for all retrial benefits including salary and allowances for the suspension period after deducting the suspension allowance paid to him.[1]

In another matter on superannuation, the period of suspension was treated on duty looking to the fact that suspension order automatically stands revoked on retirement as the relationship of master and servant has come to an end.[2]

## 3. CONSEQUENCES OF REINSTATEMENT

Reinstatement results in replacing a person in a position from which he resigned or was dismissed. It means restoration of status quo and the resignation or dismissal as the case may be, the word 're' when used as a pre-fix normally means 'again' or 'back'. Reinstatement ordinarily means restoration of ex-employee to his original post and putting him into the position he would have been if he would have continued in service all along. The word 'instatement' means that the employee is put back in the same position as if he has not been dismissed. The order of reinstatement wipes out the stagnation order of dismissal or termination. Reinstatement implies as if the order of dismissal/termination was never passed. Wherever order for reinstatement is made, two distinct consequences follow:

Firstly — Contract of service is restored.

Secondly — From the date he is entitled to wages as he was entitled to prior to the date of dismissal and the employee continues to be in service uninterrupted by the offending order. Therefore, claim for back wages is implicit and integral part and necessary inseparable concomitant of the order of reinstatement. Reinstatement can be through order of Appellate Authority or by Court/High Court etc.

In such circumstances, the demand for wages for the intervening period is raised by such reinstated employees. Supreme Court[3] has laid down the guidelines that the question of payment of the back wages is a question to be decided on the basis of

1. Bhagirathi Jena Vs Board of Directors O.S.F.C. and Others 2001(1) Bank CLR 112 (S.C.)
2. S.P. Jain Vs Punjab National Bank 1993(2) Bank CLR 12 (Delhi)
3. The Managing Director, U.P. Warehousing Corporation and Others Vs Vijai Narain Vajpai A.I.R. 1980 S.C. 840

evidence. If during the intervening period of termination and the order of the reinstatement, the employee was not working anywhere gainfully, the back wages cannot be denied.

Principle of 'no work no pay' cannot be applied in such a situation where an employee is forced and compelled to be away from his duties on a result of illegal orders of termination/dismissal.

As a consequence of setting aside of the dismissal order, reinstatement in service will be the normal rule and unless it is proved that the Delinquent Officer was gainfully employed elsewhere during the relevant period, he will be entitled to be paid the entire salary for the period during which dismissal order prevented him from earning salary. If termination/dismissal from service is held to be bad, no other punishment in the guise of denial of back wages can be imposed. However, when the Delinquent Officer has procured another employment, he will not be entitled for the back wages. Where termination is not only illegal but *void ab initio* and *non est* from its inception, the Bank on reinstatement should release all the consequential benefits as the normal rule is the payment of full back wages and the party objecting to it must establish the circumstances necessitating departure.[1] While quashing an inquiry, the High Court cannot keep the dismissal order intact on provisional basis while ordering for a fresh inquiry because an inquiry cannot be carried out against a person who is not an employee having severed relationship of master and servant by dismissal order.[2] But when Court set aside inquiry with liberty to Bank to proceed with inquiry from the stage at which infirmity occurred with reinstatement in service and payment of back wages cannot be presumed to be a condition precedent for continuing the inquiry, because the Court having permitted inquiry did not impose any condition on Bank and non-payment of salary/subsistence allowance will be a different question though the same may cause deprivation of proper opportunity to defend but inquiry can be continued.[3]

Where dismissal order passed by the management was quashed on the ground of incompetency of Disciplinary Authority, Appellate Authority and Reviewing Authority, the Delinquent Officer was deemed to be in continuous service with all consequential benefits.[4] However, when it was found that the money had been embezzled by the Delinquent Officer, he returned the money but termination orders was set aside only on technical grounds inasmuch as no inquiry was conducted, the non-awarding of back wages was held justified.[5]

1. M. Premanandanam Vs State Bank of India, Vijaiwada 1995(2) Bank CLR 157 (A.P.)
2. B.L. Kapoor Vs Allahabad Bank and Others 1996(1) Bank CLR 583 (Delhi)
3. M.C. Bhat Vs Syndicate Bank, Manipal 1996(1) Bank CLR 136
4. Shamsher Singh Vs General Manager, Personnel, Punjab and Sindh Bank/Review Authority, New Delhi 2001(1) Bank CLR 202 (Allahabad)
5. Zila Sahakari Kendriya Bank Mariyadit Vs Jagdish Chandra and Others 2001(1) Bank CLR 545 S.C.

## CHAPTER 12

# LAW RELATING TO PROBATION, TERMINATION AND RESIGNATION

1. **Termination and Simplicitor**
2. **Termination of Services on the Basis of Conviction and Moral Turpitude**
3. **Resignation**

When the master-servant relation was governed by the archaic law of hire and fire, the concept of probation in service jurisprudence was practically absent. With the advent of security in public service when termination or removal became more and more difficult and order of termination or removal from service became subject-matter of judicial review, the concept of probation came to acquire a certain connotation. If a servant could not be removed by way of punishment from service unless he is given an opportunity to meet the allegations if any against him which necessitates his removal from service, rules of natural justice postulate an inquiry into the allegations and proof thereof. This developing master-servant relationship put the master on guard. In order that an incompetent or inefficient servant is not foisted upon him because the charge of incompetence or inefficiency is easy to make but difficult to prove, concept of probation was devised. To guard against errors of human judgment in selecting suitable personnel for service, the new recruit was put on test for a period before he is absorbed in service or gets a right to the post. Period of probation gives an opportunity to the management to observe the work ability, efficiency, sincerity and competence of the probationer and if the probationer is found not suitable for the post, the management reserves a right to dispense with his service without anything more during or at the end of the prescribed period, i.e., period of probation. The law as laid down generally by Courts, is that termination of service of a probation, during or at the end of period of probation will not ordinarily, and by itself, be a punishment because the probationer so appointed has no right to continue to hold such a post any more. The period of probation, therefore, furnishes a valuable opportunity to the management to closely observe the work of probationer and by the time the period of probation expires to make up its mind whether to retain the probationer by absorbing him in regular services of the Bank or dispense with his service from the Bank. Period of probation may vary from post to post or Bank to Bank. It is not obligatory on the management of Bank to prescribe a period of probation. It is always open to management to appoint as person without putting him on probation. Power to put the officer on probation, for watching his performance; at the period during which the performance is to be observed, is the prerogative of the Bank management.

Probation implicitly connotes the idea of keeping a person on trial to assess his suitability for the post. A probationer has no right to the post until he gets confirmation. During the period of probation, it is the right of the management to judge suitability in the light of performance which if found unsatisfactory the right is inherent in the employer to terminate the probation at any time because he has not found the person suitable or that his capabilities are inadequate to measure upto the requirement of the job. In the process, necessarily an element of judgment during the period of probation is involved which cannot be anything otherwise than either reaching the conclusion that the man's performance is satisfactory or unsatisfactory. In absence of such right, the employer would be helpless in coming to a conclusion whether the employee is suitable for the organisation and is to be retained or not.

Initial appointment or promotion generally carries with it a period of probation. That means the candidate will be considered for confirmation in service subject to satisfactory report on training; passing confirmation test, if any. The period of probation in Banks is governed by a statutory provision, i.e., Service Regulations framed by Board of Directors. The initial period is generally of two years subject to certain conditions like failure to complete training satisfactorily, or passing of language test etc. For confirmation, the Competent Authority must satisfactorily form an opinion.

Further, Bank may impose any other test as per its requirement, verbal or written in its Service Regulations. In a case where Board of Directors provided a confirmation test without amending the relevant Service Regulations, the same was treated as a variation in the service condition laid down by Service Regulations[1] and accordingly provision was struck down.

Deemed confirmation which is inferred from the employer's conduct is permissible only when it follows from the positive act of the employer permitting the employee

---

1. Khar Bhan Ram Vs General Manager, Punjab National Bank, 1993(2) Bank CLR 109

to continue to work on the post even after completion of the maximum period of probation permitted under the service rules; since no other inference will be possible in such a situation from the employer's conduct of continuing to take work from the employee after that period. However, when service rules permits continuance in service as a probationer beyond a certain period, an express order of confirmation is necessary to give the employee a substantive right to the post and the mere fact that he is allowed to continue in the post after the specified period of probation will not be sufficient for deeming him comfirmed.[1]

*During the probation period, an assessment of work should be there. The probationer should be made aware of the defect in his work and deficiency in his performance.* Timely communication of the assessment of work puts the probationer on right track. Without any such communication, it may be arbitrary to give a movement order to the probationer on the ground of unsuitability and an order of termination or discharge will be held violated being colourable exercise of power.

*During the probation period, the services are terminable with one month's notice or emoluments in lieu thereof.* Probation period can be extended by management in its discretion. When Service Regulations of Bank provide period of extension of probation, the probation cannot be extended beyond that period. On expiry of probation/extended period, the Competent Authority either has to terminate the services within the extended period or to confirm the service. Regulations cast an obligation upon the Competent Authority to take a decision either way. Such Regulation is mandatory in nature. Exercise of power to extend the probation is hedged with the existence of the rule in that regard followed by positive act of either confirmation of the probation or discharge from service or reversion to the substantive post within a reasonable time after the expiry of the period of probation. If the rules do not empower the appointing authority to extend the prescribed period, then inaction on the part of management for a long time may lead to an indication of the satisfactory completion of probation.[2] Thus, where an officer of a Gramin Bank was allowed to continue around fifty days less than three years, he was deemed to have been confirmed by implication.[3]

On promotion also, the prescription of two years period of training and probation is found sometimes. It is neither statutory nor has any binding force under Industrial Law. It is product of long practice. On promotion, the period of probation cannot be different for direct recruitees and promotees because it will be violation of Articles 14 and 16 of The Constitution of India.

So far as *termination of Service during Probation* is concerned, though a charge-sheet might have been pending yet the employee having been informed of his

1. Chief General Manager, State Bank of India and Another Vs Bijoy Kumar Misra 1997(2) Bank CLR 617 S.C.
2. Municipal Corporation Raipur Vs Ashok Kumar Mishra 1991(3) S.C.C. 325
3. Swatantra Kumar Singh Vs Gorakhpur Kshetriya Gramin Bank and Others 2000(3) Bank CLR 30 (Allahabad)

unsatisfactory performance by extending probation period for two times was held sufficient material for passing an order of termination simplicitor.[1]

Where an officer under probation was served with termination letter stating *"performance has not come up to the expected standards and also that her attendance record is not satisfactory. It has been decided to terminate the services during the period of probation"*, it was held that the order carries with it stigma and was likely to cause prejudice to a future employer and therefore it cannot be treated as a termination *simplicitor*.[2] Order for termination *simplicitor* should be such that if shown to a future employer it should not prejudice him against the employee on the ground that he/she had been turned out of the earlier service for some mistake or incompetence. Any order containing allegations of misconduct can be made only when a charge-sheet has been issued on the ground of misconduct.

But when notice is given to employee as to why his services should not be terminated and conduct of employee is unsatisfactory, any confirmation by implication is negativated.[3]

Lastly, we may refer to the law laid down by the Supreme Court of India[4] that a probationer has no right to hold the post and his service can be terminated at any time during or at the end of the period of probation on account of general suitability for the post held by him. If the Competent Authority holds an inquiry for judging the suitability of the probationer or for his further continuation in service or for confirmation and such inquiry is the basis for taking decision to terminate his service, then the action of the Competent Authority cannot be castigated as punitive. However, if the allegation of misconduct constitutes the foundation of the action taken, the ultimate decision taken by the Competent Authority can be nullified on the ground of violation of the rules of natural justice.

## 1. TERMINATION AND SIMPLICITOR

If an employee loses the confidence, the management cannot be compelled to allow the employee to continue under it. If the management decides to discontinue the service without attaching any stigma and in accordance with the rules governing the conditions of employment in that event, the same cannot be said to be a penalty in disguise if the rules of employment permits dispensation of service on certain conditions.

Under Service Regulations, there are necessarily provisions for termination wherein an employee in services can be terminated with immediate effect by giving a three months salary or by serving a three months notice. Such terminations are made sparingly, generally in public interest. The question whether termination simplicitor

1. The Royal Seema Grameena Bank Kuddapah Vs D. Pattabhiramudu 1995(2) Bank CLR 47 A.P
2. Suman Lata Agrawal Vs Union Bank of India 1988(2) Bank CLR 373
3. Samsher Singh Vs State of Punjab 1974(2) S.C.C. 831
4. State Bank of India and Others Vs Palak Modi and Another A.I.R. 2013 S.C. (Civil) 566

is an innocuous order is in terms of contract of service and the Service Rules or solely the product of desire to inflict a punishment is a matter to be decided with reference to the each case. A mere other motive or motives which might exist in the employer at the time of termination would not itself make the order when if it is otherwise in terms of appointment or conditions of service but where it is found that such motive has matured to become the foundation of the order, the order will become bad.

Thus, where management finds that without going to the question of misconduct the services can be terminated because of otherwise unsatisfactory performance of officer employee or for his unsuitability or inadequacy to the job and in termination order if the fact is indicated that the employee is under suspension, then it will be only by way of describing him as under suspension but it will not be treated as stigma.

However, when an employee is given extension of service beyond the age of superannuation for a specified period, he acquires a right to hold the post during the said period. Any premature termination of service before the expiry of the period of extension has to be done for good reasons and after complying with the 'principles of natural justice.'[1]

As per Service Regulation, a Bank Officer can be compulsorily retired at the discretion of Competent Authority by giving him three months notice in writing but such power should be exercised where such retirement is either deemed desirable or in the interest of the Bank. Where an order of retirement did not contain any averment that it has been considered desirable in the interest of the Bank, to retire an officer, the order was struck down by the Court.[2] Such order has to be in accordance with service regulation of the Bank.

## 2. TERMINATION OF SERVICES ON THE BASIS OF CONVICTION AND MORAL TURPITUDE

*Moral turpitude* is not defined in the Banking Regulation Act or in any other penal statute. Any thing contrary to justice, honesty, modesty or good morals is defined as such.

By and large, it refers to moral character and state of mind. Being vague term, its meaning depends on the state of public morals. The acts of baseness, vileness or depravity in the private and social duties which a man owes to his fellowmen or to society in general, contrary to the accepted and customary rule of right and duty between man and man will imply in the definition. It also implies something immoral in itself regardless of the fact whether it is punishable by law.

In Black's Law Dictionary, 5th Edition, it is defined as the quality of a crime involving grave infringement of the moral sentiment of the community as distinguished from statutory malafides. The test to judge certain act should be—

1. Hariday Chaitanya Biswas and Others Vs State Bank of India and Others 1990(2) Bank CLR 127
2. Surendra Pratap Singh Kushvaha Vs State Bank of Indore 1988(1) Bank CLR 413

I. Whether the offence punished was of such a nature which will shock the moral conscience of society in general.

II. Whether the offender can be considered to be of a person of depraved character or a person was to be looked down by the society.

Meaning of word 'Moral' defers from individual to individual at a given point of time. The meaning to word moral has undergone change and acquired different connotations at different times at different stages of social evolution, development and growth. It is not a static concept. As a legal term, moral turpitude can be defined as a quality of crime involving grave infringement of the moral sentiment of the community as distinguished from statutory *'mala-prohibita'*.

Every false statement if discloses vileness or depravity in the doing of any private and social duty to the society or fellowmen will be moral turpitude. Where an officer of Bank was guilty of forcibly removing his son from the custody of his wife and was declared guilty for contempt of Court in that he had failed to produce the child even after an order was passed in that regard by High Court, it was held[1] that the offence of contempt of Court did involve moral turpitude and dismissal was held justified.

Under Section 10 of The Banking Regulation Act, there are restrictions on banking company to employ or to continue in employment of any person.

Section 10 of Banking Regulation Act, 1949 runs as under—

*"Prohibition of employment of managing agents and restrictions on certain forms of employment—*

(1) No banking company—

(a) shall employ or be managed by a managing agent; or

(b) shall employ or continue the employment of any person—

(i) who is, or at any time has been, adjudicated insolvent, or has suspended payment or has compounded with his creditors, or who is, or has been, convicted by a criminal court of an offence involving moral turpitude; or

(ii) whose remuneration or part of whose remuneration takes the form of commission or of a share in the profits of the company:

[1][Provided that nothing contained in this sub-clause shall apply to the payment by a banking company of—

(a) any bonus in pursuance of a settlement or award arrived at or made under any law relating to industrial disputes or in accordance with any scheme framed by such banking company or in accordance with the usual practice prevailing in banking business;

1. Captain Dushyant Somal Vs Governor RBI Bombay 1991(1) Bank CLR 402

(b) any commission to any broker (including guarantee broker), cashier-contractor, clearing and forwarding agent, auctioneer or any other person, employed by the banking company under a contract otherwise than as a regular member of the staff of the company; or]

(iii) whose remuneration is, in the opinion of the Reserve Bank, excessive; or

(c) shall be managed by any person—

[2][(i) who is a director of any other company not being—

(a) a subsidiary of the banking company, or

(b) a company registered under Section 25 of the Companies Act, 1956 (1 of 1956):

provided that the prohibition in this sub-clause shall not apply in respect of any such director for a temporary period not exceeding three months or such further period not exceeding nine months as the Reserve Bank may allow; or]

(ii) who is engaged in any other business or vocation; or

(iii) [3][whose .....”

It is a disqualifying clause. The section disqualifies an employee from continuing in service the moment he is convicted of an offence involving moral turpitude.

In tune with the above provisions of law, Service Regulations of different banks provide a procedure of termination who has been convicted of a charge of moral turpitude. On account of conviction by Criminal Court on criminal charge, the action is necessary under the Conduct/Service Regulations of a Bank. Here, the strength of termination order flows out of conclusion arrived at by a judicial trial. There is no need that the charge leveled in Court must constitute misconduct under Conduct Regulations.[1]

Supreme Court's settled view is that any Rule providing for termination of services of employees involved in criminal cases without holding inquiry, subject to result of criminal trial, is not violative of Articles 14 and 21 of the Constitution.

Further, merely because sentence is suspended or the accused is released on bail, the conviction order does not cease to be operative. In Bipartite Agreement for award staff also, Clause 19.2 provides *"by the expression 'offence' shall be meant any offence involving moral turpitude for which an employee is liable to conviction and sentence under any provision of law."*

Penal statutes distinguish between intentional and unintentional acts; death caused by rash and negligent driving does not involve moral turpitude but a deliberate

1. S. Vasundhara Vs Canara Bank 7 and Others 1997(1) Bank CLR 315 (S.C.)

intention to kill another one drives and the act will become involving moral turpitude. Though the act and the result of the act may be the same in both, the main and important difference between the two is the lack of intention in the former and the presence of it in the later.

Finally, the question whether a particular offence involves moral turpitude or moral delinquency has to be examined on the facts of each matter. It is not merely the section of offence which matters such. Facts on which the offence is made out have also some bearing on the answer to the question.[1] Whether an offence under Section 138 of Negotiable Instrument Act will constitute an offence involving moral turpitude, it was held[2] that a cause of action for a criminal prosecution under Section 138 of the Negotiable Instrument Act will arise, not on the date of issuance of the cheque, but only when the drawer of the cheque fails to pay the amount on demand within the statutory period. A person may issue cheque with insufficient funds expecting arrangement on the date of its presentment. Therefore, whether such an offence will involve moral turpitude only when the element of cheating exists and thus an offence of issuance of a cheque without sufficient funds will not be moral turpitude unless the offence is also covered under Section 415 of Indian Penal Code. However, when in a case under Section 138 of N.I. Act, a convicted Bank employee filed a revision petition in High Court and made payment of cheque amount and Court allowed complainant to compound the offence under Section 320 Cr PC. The foundation of order of termination being incorrect because the employee at no point of time compounded the offence with the creditor as laid down in Section 10(i)(b), the same was set aside.[3]

Similarly, a conviction under Section 304 Cr PC or 304 (A) IPC will not come under definition of moral turpitude though initially charge might have been framed under Section 302 Indian Penal Code.[4]

In another case where even punishment under disciplinary enquiry has been ordered but conviction order comes afterwards on the same charge, the order of termination has to be passed. The special procedure provided in the Conduct Regulation of Bank is required to be followed.[5]

Again where by reducing the punishment of discharge from service, the Appellate Authority reduce the punishment to stoppage of five future increments with cumulative effect but afterwards, under criminal proceedings a sentence to one month and to undergo fifteen days simple imprisonment in case of default in payment of fine was awarded and termination of services on the basis of sentences under Section 10(1)(B) of the Banking Regulation Act was found to be legal and valid regardless of the punishment in Disciplinary Action/Proceedings.[6]

---

1. Joy Vs State of Kerala 1991 K.L.T. 153
2. Saseendran Nair Vs General Manager 1997(1) Bank CLR 318
3. P.R. Kamath Vs Indian Bank 2003(3) Bank CLR 532 (Kant)
4. S. Noor Ahmed Vs State Bank of India 1993(2) Bank CLR 9
5. Shib Nath Bodhak Vs Bank of India 2001(3) Bank CLR 339 (Cal.)
6. G. Greesan Vs Indian Overseas Bank 1994(1) Bank CLR 205 (Kerala)

The position that the Delinquent Officer is under suspension without any pay as per orders of Court will not make the situation different and plea of no prejudice to management will not prevail.[1]

When an employee charged with serious criminal offence under the Indian Penal Code has already been convicted by appropriate Criminal Court, mere pendency of an appeal cannot operate as a bar to proceed against him in terms of the show cause notice issued against him. If he is subsequently acquitted by the Court of Appeal, he has remedy if he suffers from any order of dismissal in the meantime.

However, such termination order can be reviewed/revised by Bank in suitable cases. Thus, in a case, refusal of Bank to reconsider the case being under Section 12 of Probation of Offenders Act was held bad. Because according to Section 12 of Probation of Offenders Act, no disqualification can be attached to the employee on account of his conviction.[2]

The special procedure in cases of conviction provided in Conduct Regulation of Bank cannot be applied where though the employee has been acquitted of the criminal charges but certain observations have occurred in the judgment regarding negligence of the employee. The reason being that since the Delinquent Officer was acquitted of all the charges, there will remain no occasion for him to prefer an appeal for challenging the correctness and propriety of the observations relating to his alleged negligence of duty.

When an employee is terminated after inquiry, then exoneration from Court in criminal proceedings will not weigh because under Disciplinary Action/Proceedings a conclusion different from that arrives at by the Court may be arrived at and termination based on findings cannot be disturbed.[3]

A special procedure has been envisaged under Conduct Regulations for imposing any of the major penalties and it is not necessary to conduct an inquiry since the Disciplinary Action proceeds on the basis of findings of Courts but Conduct Regulations mandates that the employee be given an opportunity of making representation on the penalty proposed/imposed.

On receipt of a conviction order, the next step will be to ensure that the received order is true and certified copy of the judgment of the Court. A study of the judgment will show whether the charges leveled have been held to be proved by the Court concerned. Though Court might not have awarded any punishment, still merely conviction or declaring the accused as offender will be sufficient to take action under the relevant Regulation of the Bank provided the matter otherwise falls in it. After receiving conviction order, a show cause notice will be issued as to why the services

---

1. Dina Bandhu Mondal Vs Bank of India 2002(1) Bank CLR 71 (Calcutta)
2. Zonal Manager and Disciplinary Authority, Indian Bank and Another Vs Parupurredy Satyanarayana 1990(1) Bank CLR 329
3. Allahabad District Co-operative Bank Ltd., Allahabad Vs Vidya Varidh Mishra 2005(1) Bank CLR 93 (S.C.)

of the concerned employee should not be terminated in view of Regulation/Bipartite Settlement. After considering the reply, if any, submitted by the concerned employee necessary orders will be passed. In case no reply is received, termination order will be passed. Since it will be a case of termination simplicitor, it will be proper if a cheque of equivalent to the salary of three months is enclosed alongwith such order. After that, in due course, terminal dues of the dismissed employee can be released.

Now, the question arises what is the position when an employee is acquitted honourably or on the ground of benefit of doubt by Court. An acquittal does not automatically give the employee the right to be reinstated in service. It will be still open to management to take decision whether the Delinquent Officer should be taken back in service or Disciplinary Action/Proceedings should be started under Conduct Regulations. Thus, before reinstatement, the decision will be whether the employee should be kept under suspension or not.

So far as reinstatement of such person on being acquitted in appeal is concerned, Supreme Court[1] has held that if such person succeeds in appeal or other proceedings, the matter can be reviewed in such a manner so that he may not suffer prejudice.

## 3. RESIGNATION

Resignation in relation to an office means the act of giving up or relinquishment or to loose hold of the office. Therefore, it means that the employee wants to sever his relation from the employer without any riders and then only it would amount to resignation. It is characteristically the voluntarily surrender of a position by the one resigning made freely and not under duress. The word is defined generally as meaning the act of resigning or giving up as a claim possession or position. Resignation is spontaneous relinquishment of one's own right. It becomes effective when the authority competent to make appointment accept it. Unless the employee is relieved from duty after acceptance of the offer of voluntary retirement or resignation, jural relationship of the employee and the employer does not come to an end.[2]

It is not obligatory on the part of management to convey its acceptance within the period of notice, i.e., within three months though the rules may provide for acceptance within three months. Delay in communication of acceptance of resignation is to be treated as procedural and will not be treated to have vitiated the acceptance itself.[3]

Acceptance of resignation and waiving of the period of notice or salary in lieu thereof is not a simple administrative function but it amounts to acting on behalf of the Bank. Therefore, competent/delegate authorities cannot further delegate the powers conferred upon them in absence of a specific authority to some delegate. Where an authority is not competent, accepts the resignation, the act cannot be ratified

1. Dy. Director of Collegiate Education (Admn.), Madras Vs Nagoor Meera A.I.R. 1995 S.C. 1365
2. State Bank of Patiala Vs Phoolpati 2005(3) Bank CLR 67 (S.C.)
3. H.C. Jain Vs State Bank of India and Others 1998(1) Bank CLR 507 (Raj)

by the competent authority because ratification can only be made of a irregular or voidable act but not of void and without jurisdiction act.[1] A responsible employee cannot seek to set himself free from the responsibilities of his office by early flinging on the management a letter evincing his desire to exit from employment. To permit officials unilaterally to throw away, the apparel of authority would generate hectic condition in sensitive areas particularly in banking industry where certainty is rightly mandated. The employee of bank cannot adopt an attitude that his office is just another piece of abandoned baggage. But Bank cannot initiate Disciplinary Action/Proceedings for absence after submission of Voluntary Retirement application with the purpose of stopping Voluntary Retirement.[2]

Refusal of Voluntary Retirement was held justified when a notice was issued calling explanation for the lapses on the part of the officer and the plea of employee that no Disciplinary Action/Proceedings is contemplated against merely because the notice calling for explanation does not contain the language "to show cause as to why Disciplinary Action/Proceedings be not initiated" was not found to favour with the Court.[3]

However, where an officer employee opted for pension but on retirement came to know that his petition for pension for exercise of pension option was not considered, the Bank took stand that no such petition was received either in Zonal office or in Head office and as such the case of the employee was not considered for pension but High Court observed that though the pension option might not have been received at Zonal Office/Head Office but for the latches on the part of the employees of the Bank the pension optee cannot be made suffer.[4]

The procedure of quitting the employment has been canalised banking industry. These are two methods for quitting the job—

1. Resignation
2. Quitting job under some scheme like Voluntary Retirement

There are special provisions in Service Regulation which allow employees to quit the job with previous permission of management. The main difference between a resignation and VRS application are as under:

1. Every employee has right to resign but only eligible employee can apply for Voluntary retirement under Service Rules.
2. In case of Disciplinary Action/Proceedings, the VRS application may not be considered at all or it will be considered within the rules but in case

---

1. Hardwari Lal Vs Union of India through Secretary Ministry of Finance, New Delhi 1990(2) Bank CLR 243
2. Ramdas Somaji Nikam Vs Indian Bank 2001(3) Bank CLR 81 (Bombay)
3. S.K. Bangia Vs State Bank of India 1996(1) Bank CLR 190 (Delhi)
4. Kishun Lall Vs Chairman and Managing Director, UCO Bank and Others 2003(1) Bank CLR 288 (Patna)

of resignation. There is prohibitive prohibition against an officer subjected to Disciplinary Action/Proceedings under Conduct Regulation. Resignation is a right of an employee while VRS is a concession on the part of management.

3. The VRS application can be rejected by management without assigning any reason.

4. In case of resignation, the employee receives only statutory dues but in case of Voluntary Retirement, he will receive all the normal superannuation benefits, subject to rules of the Bank.

   Sometimes, VRS schemes are funded schemes, normally called golden handshake schemes. Under such schemes, time is given to every employee to opt for voluntary retirement and similarly time is given to management to work out the scheme. Creation of funds depends upon number of applications, liability which the scheme would impose on Bank which is variable factors. VRS does not have any statutory force though the same is a policy decision on the part of Bank and Government. Such schemes are not framed in exercise of powers under Section 19 of Banking Companies Act (5 of 1970) general power under Section 7(2) of the Act. Even if scheme provides that employee having once applied cannot seek cancellation, does effect the right in law to withdraw application for premature retirement.

   In the Bank of India case,[1] two questions arose whether the scheme is an offer or an invitation inviting offer and secondly whether the optees having accepted the benefits under the scheme could be permitted to resile therefrom.

   On the first question, the verdict was that the scheme is contractual in nature and constituted an invitation and not an offer as no consideration passed in terms of scheme so as to constitute agreement and that revocation was possible at any time before acceptance as up to such an acceptance no legal obligation existed.

   On the second question, it was held that those employees who have therefore accepted the payments/benefits under the scheme cannot approbate and reprobate nor cannot be permitted to withdraw. Again Supreme Court reiterated[2] its view by holding that anyone who knowingly accepts the benefits of a contract is estopped from denying the binding effect on him of such contract.

5. Resignation can be accepted by the appointing authority or above while rules describing the nature of Voluntary Retirement and scope of Voluntary

1. Bank of India Vs O.P. Swarnkar 2003(2) S.C.C. 721
2. Punjab and Sindh Bank Vs S. Ranveer Singh Bawa 2004(2) Bank CLR 35 (S.C.)

Retirement, Allahabad High Court[1] summarised the main features of Voluntary Retirement as under:

"I . *Relinquishment of an office by voluntary retirement is bilateral and employee can retire only if his option is accepted.*

II. *An employee may withdraw his option of voluntary retirement before it becomes effective or in other words relationship of employer and employee comes to an end.*

III. *But the said right (to withdraw the option of voluntary retirement) is subject to any lawful restriction.*"

Where a resignation is submitted by a manager stating that he is submitting it due to frustration caused by false allegations by Chairman and withdrew the same the very same day but Chairman accepted the resignation and refused to revoke it.[2] The order was held inconsistent with law and appeal of employees was allowed.

Ground of management exigency may be there but resignation cannot be wiped without a cogent reason except in case where Disciplinary Action/Proceedings is pending. Actually, the resignation of an employee from service, being a voluntary act on the part of an employee, he is entitled to choose the date with effect from which his resignation would be effective and give a notice to the employer accordingly. The only restriction is that the proposed date should not be earlier than three months from the date on which the notice is given of the proposed resignation. Though there may be no specific provision in the Regulations permitting the employee to withdraw the resignation still he can withdraw as a general rule. Therefore, in some Banks, this right of withdrawal is also made subject to the permission of the employer.[3]

While we compare 'resignation' with retirement, the two words convey totally different meanings in common parlance. An employee can resign at any point of time, even on the second day of his appointment but in case of retirement he retires only after attaining the age of superannuation or in case of voluntary retirement on completion of qualifying service. Resignation brings about complete cessation of master and servant relationship whereas voluntary retirement maintains the relationship for the purpose of grant of retrial benefits in view of the part service.

1. Smt. Rajni Jain Vs Punjab and Sindh Bank and Another 2001(2) Bank CLR 216 (Allahabad)
2. Phool Chand Sung Vs Chairman, Vindhyavasini Gramin Bank and Others 2006(3) Bank CLR 8(
3. Punjab National Bank Vs P.K. Mittal 1989(2) Bank CLR 29

# CHAPTER 13

# MISCELLANEOUS MATTERS

1. **Transfer**
2. **Prosecution Sanction**
3. **Pre-appointment Matters**

## 1. TRANSFER

Transfer means movement from one centre to another and transferability means every officer is liable for transfer to any office or branch of the Bank or to any place in India. Generally, officers are liable for transfer on completion of the tenure.

An order of transfer is an incidence of service. Who should be transferred, and where, is a matter for the appropriate authority to decide. Unless the order of transfer is vitiated by malafide or is made in violation of any statutory provisions, the same will not be liable to be challenged. There is always a presumption that the official action is reasonable and in public interest. It is for challenging party to discharge its burden for showing that reasonableness is wanted or conformity with public interest is not there. The onus on the person who alleges malafide in transfer is very heavy. The Court will not interfere with it. Order of transfers passed on administrative grounds and in ordinary course will not be liable to be set aside by Courts of law. The transfer is an incidence of service. This power is inherent to an employer.

It is a fact that order of transfer often causes a lot of difficulties and dislocation in the family set-up of the concerned employee but on this score the same cannot be set aside. In a transferable post, an order of transfer is a normal consequence and personal difficulties are matters for consideration of management.

Transfer is a necessary concomitant of every service. Therefore, if the administrative exigencies warrant a transfer, the Courts will not exercise their jurisdiction. The mere fact that employee was subjected to three transfers or it had come in the middle of the year will be of no consequence. Even policy adumbrated in a circular could not be enforced because these circulars are intended only for internal guidance.[1] The reason for transfer if *per se* appears justified and the nature of transfer causes minimum inconvenience to the employee, the inference should be drawn that the act of transfer is legitimate to meet administrative requirements. Any order to transfer made in pursuance of general toning up of the administration cannot be said to be malafide. The guidelines framed for transfer of an employee do not confer a legally enforceable right upon the employee to challenge the order of transfer which has been made to satisfy administrative exigencies. But any such breach may come in aid of establishing a transfer to be malafide.[2]

Where guidelines for transfer policy provided that the officers who have crossed 55 years of age shall ordinarily be exempted from the purview of policy, the Court held that there is no bar for transfer for an officer who has crossed the age of 55 years. Word 'ordinarily' means only 'as far as possible'.[3]

Ordinarily and or for practicable purpose, the husband and wife who are both employed should be posted at the same station even if their employers are different. The definability of such a course is obvious. But it does not mean that invariably they should be posted at the same station. While choosing the carrier and a particular service, the couple has to bear in mind this factor and be prepared to face such a hardship.

If administrative needs and transfer policy do not permit the posting of both at one place without sacrificing of the requirements of administration, the couple have to make their choice at the threshold between carrier prospects and family life.[4] Thus, posting both husband and wife, be at the same station, cannot be claimed as of right. Generally, the Bank management is entitled to decide on a consideration of the necessities of business, whether the transfer of an employee should be made to a particular branch.

Only management is in the best position to judge how to distribute its employees between the different branches taking the view that interference by court with day-to-day transfer order will create chaos in the administration which cannot be conducive to public interest. Whenever transfer order is given, it must be complied and in case of genuine difficulty representation to Competent Authority should be made and in case transfer order is not stayed/modified, the same must be carried out. There is

---

1. Syndicate Bank Vs Sunder K. Paniyade 1992(1) L.L.J. 273
2. Bhanu Prasad Vs State Bank of Bikaner and Jaipur and Others 1990(1) Bank CLR 84 (H.C. M.P. Indore Bench)
3. Dr. M.V. Rao Vs Chief General Manager, State Bank of India and Another 2001(1) Bank CLR 579
4. Bank of India Vs Jagjit Singh Mehata; A.I.R. 1992 S.C. 519, 1992(1) Bank CLR 399

no justification for an officer to avoid or evade a transfer order merely on the ground having made a representation or the ground of his difficulty in moving from one place to another. Where Branch Manager filed writ on the ground of non-availability of treatment in specialty services, the High Court refused to interfere and directed the employee to submit his representation at new place of posting highlighting his grievances.[1]

Therefore, when a transfer policy of Bank provides for different transfer norms between direct recruitees and promotees (promoted from award staff), no hostile discrimination can be found in such classification being reasonable one.[2]

But where transfer order suffers from the vice of apparent malafide or violates any statute, the same can be interfered with by the courts. When transfer orders are made by an authority that has no competency or the motive of transfer is to victimise the employee or made with malafide intention, the court can interfere. Where the employee was not given even seven days time to join his transferred post, it was held[3] that there is a serious doubt about the bonafide exercise of the power of the transfer.

It is well settled principle that unless in the court it is established that an order of transfer is on the fact of malafide and was not in interest of administration and/ or is violative of any of the rules of transfer or the like, the validity of the order of transfer cannot be challenged. Union leader cannot claim any preferential treatment or any immunity from transfer. Similarly, an employee cannot complain that his transfer from one place to another would prevent him from carrying on his trade union activities. There is no special privilege for a trade unionist unless there is some circular or rules of the Bank. Thus, when a question of transfer is to be examined, such employee shall be viewed as a regular employee only. In such a situation, such a high degree of prejudice is not caused which would automatically lead to an inference that the act of transfer has been malafide.[4] A discrimination cannot be made between an employee who is not a union leader and employee who is a union leader. Under our constitution, an employee has trade union right subject to conditions and restrictions.

But transfer cannot be made for punishing an employee of Bank. It should not be punitive in nature. It is not as if an erring employee had to be tolerated by an institution. If there are any specific incidents of misconduct, they can certainly be enquired into in a dispassionate manner.

Subjecting an employee to harassment of one kind or the other would not add to the credibility of the institution. Therefore, where Bank failed to take into

---

1. Ajay Kumar Das Vs State Bank of India and Others 2006(1) Bank CLR 504 (Orissa)
2. Banshi Lal Chandel and Others Vs Union Bank of India, Bombay 1997(1) Bank CLR 422 (Allahabad)
3. Bhanu Prasad Vs State Bank of Bikaner and Jaipur and Others 1990(1) Bank CLR 84 (H.C. M.P. Indore Bench)
4. Basanta Kumar Roy Vs IDBI Bank Ltd. and Others 2010 (2) DRT Cases 42 (Calcutta High Court)

consideration of medical problems and posting of a woman employee's husband, the transfer orders were set aside.[1] Where in reply to representation for cancellation of transfer, the officer was informed that his transfer had been made in view of his unsatisfactory performance the transfer was declared punitive and cancelled.[2]

On the amalgamation of New Bank of India with Punjab National Bank, unions of NBI challenged the mass-scale transfer before Allahabad High Court amongst others on the ground that transfer policy was bad being discriminating for NBI employees by treating them surplus. Supreme Court while reversing the judgment of single judge and division bench found that no discrimination has been made. The mass transfers are not rotational transfers but in the nature of redeployment of surplus staff. Therefore, guidelines issued by the management of NBI will not be applicable. Accordingly, the transfer orders were upheld.[3]

Where an officer approached Court assailing his transfer order on the ground that impugned transfer order will result in obstruction of his career path because he will not be able to complete rural stint. Court refused to interfere in absence of any malafide or breach of any statutory rule.[4] Considering that continued hospitalization is not necessary for the mentally retarded son of the employee, the same was not considered as good ground for disturbing the transfer made by the Bank in view of transfer policy of the Bank.[5] Where transfer made to maintain peace in office because the female colleagues complained of sexual harassment, the same was protected by holding that there is no penal consequences or adverse impact and intention of management to maintain peace, cannot be said to be an irrelevant consideration for transfer.[6]

The malafide or colourable exercise of powers or oblique motives of the authority concerned are to be presumed from all the facts and circumstances relevant to a particular action of transfer. Malafide or oblique motives are not visible objects but are visible through the mind by formulating an impression putting all relevant facts and circumstances together which will give rise to an action.[7]

The transfer orders issued in a private bank cannot be challenged in a writ petition because the employee's rights are neither fundamental rights nor the statutory ones.[8]

---

1. Bookarupanda Padmavathi Vs Bank of India, Vishakhapatnam 2008(3) Bank CLR 413 (Andhra Pradesh)
2. A.K. Chakraborty Vs New Bank of India and Others 1993(2) Bank CLR 363
3. Punjab National Bank and Others Vs All India N.B.I. Employees Federation and Others 1999(1) Bank CLR 41
4. Basant Kumar Singh Vs State Bank of India 2004(1) Bank CLR 386 (Patna)
5. J.P. Sharma Vs State Bank of India and Others 2002(2) Bank CLR 194 (Del)
6. NABARD, Calcutta Vs Dibanker Sen Roy 2009(2) Bank CLR 149 (Cal)
7. Sailendra Kumar Saran Vs Syndicate Bank 2001(2) Bank CLR 2 (Calcutta)
8. Subrata Bhowmik Vs Bharat Overseas Bank Ltd. and Others 2001(1) Bank CLR 418 (Calcutta)

## 2. PROSECUTION SANCTION

Whenever a first information report is lodged and on an investigation CBI/Police agency finds that an offence has been committed, a request is made by CBI/Police agency to Bank for according sanction to prosecute the employee. It is done under Section 19 of Prevention of Corruption Act, 1988. At the time of according sanction to prosecute, what is required to be seen is; whether there is sufficient material on record to accord sanction so that an accused can be dealt with in accordance with law or not, whether there is sufficient evidence or enough material to show 'dishonest intention' or 'participation' to establish the charge or to prove the guilt, though such questions can be decided finally at the stage of trial only.

Where Bank Executive Committee firstly declined to accord sanction for prosecution but Central Vigilance Commission did not agree and directed Bank to accord sanction, later on Bank granted sanction to CBI for prosecution. The employee raised the plea that Bank does not have power to review its earlier decision. Gujarat High Court[1] turned down the plea by holding that it is an administrative action and therefore opens for review. Granting of prosecution sanction is not a final decision of any kind; therefore the question of affording opportunity of hearing to the employee will not arise.

## 3. PRE-APPOINTMENT MATTERS

It is well established that inclusion of name in the list of successful candidates does not confer an indefeasible right to be appointed. The notification/declaration merely amounts to an invitation to qualified candidates to apply for recruitment and on their selection they do not acquire any right to the post. Unless the relevant recruitment rules so indicate the State/the employer is not under legal duty to fill up all or any of the vacancies.[2]

Therefore, when a select list candidate occupying 47th position filed a writ claiming for appointment while the penal stood expired as one year passed and NABARD refused to extend the life of panel of candidates but a few persons were appointed, awaiting instructions of NABARD after one year, the Supreme Court dismissed the writ due the candidate not having any legal right and further in view that even if the Bank would have been asked to act in terms of select list, it would have been obligated to appoint only those persons whose names appear higher on the list.[3]

However when a promise is made to give appointment by an Institution to somebody, it is binding for the Institution to keep its promise and issue appointment letter as assured and promised. Unless there are circumstances justifying refusal, the appointment cannot be withdrawn.

---

1. Durga Prasad P. Dash Vs State Bank of Saurashtra 1996(2) Bank CLR 171 (Gujarat)
2. Shankarsan Dash Vs Union of India 1991(1) S.C.C. 471, 1991 AIR S.C. 1583
3. Aryavart Gramin Bank Vs Vijay Shankar Shukla 2008(1) Bank CLR 90 (S.C.)

An officer of Tripura Gramin Bank cleared the selection process conducted by State Bank of India and was issued a letter that he has been selected for probationary officer of State Bank of India. The letter also stated that his selection was subject to completion of necessary formalities and further communication will be given by State Bank of India shortly. But State Bank of India later on refused on the basis of adverse reports of referees which reported about irregularities committed by the officer as drawing of false

TA Bill in Tripura Gramin Bank. Meanwhile the officer employee also submitted his resignation from Tripura Gramin Bank and release orders were issued. *Relying on the principle of promissory estoppels, the Court held that equitable estoppels would require that a person, who has acted to his detriment induced by an expectation, would be protected so that* an injustice may not be perpetrated. The promise of an appointment made by the Bank being intended to be legally binding and to be acted upon and it having been acted by the employee was binding on the Bank. State Bank of India was directed to issue fresh appointment letter.[1] In another example where an employee officer of the Bank was selected to the post of Assistant Provident Fund Commissioner by UPSC and appointment letter was issued setting out the terms and conditions of appointment but his resignation in Bank was not accepted due to pendency of Disciplinary Action/Proceedings and Bank refused to issue No Objection Certificate; resultantly, the offer of appointment by UPSC was cancelled. In writ filed by the officer, it was held that merely because Disciplinary Action/Proceedings has come to an end during the period and there no financial liability is to be discharged, it cannot be made ground for issuing appointment letter.[2]

The reason being that the officer was awarded punishment in inquiry and that now even if an integrity certificate is issued, then same will necessarily contain this blot of punishment namely, withholding of one increment with cumulative effect and therefore the department cannot be made to suffer a person who does not have good antecedents.

Where caste certificate, on the basis whereof the employee got employment, was false resulting in termination of services on the report of Scrutiny Committee, the same was challenged in Court by the employee. The Supreme Court held[3] that appointment wrongly obtained on the basis of false social status certificate necessarily has the effect of depriving the genuine scheduled caste/scheduled tribe or other backward class candidates.

The plea regarding rendering services for a long period on the basis, false caste certificate has been considered and rejected in a series of decisions, *Equity, sympathy*

1. Bidhan Chandra Chakma Vs Chief General Manager State Bank of India North Eastern Circle and Others 1988(1) Bank CLR 69
2. Central Provident Fund Commissioner and Others Vs Ashok Dubey and Others 1993(1) Bank CLR 151
3. Regional Manager Central Bank of India Vs Madhulika Guru Prasad Dahir and Others 2009(1) Bank CLR 381 (S.C.)

*or generosity has no place where the original appointment rests on a false caste certificate* and such appointment cannot be recognised and regularised regardless of the fact of long services rendered by the employee.

Though an appointment letter was containing the language, "if any declaration/ statement or information given by him/her is at any time found to be false or untrue or if any material particular is suppressed, his/her services are liable to be terminated forthwith without any notice or compensation in lieu thereof" yet the interpretation of clause was that the word "found to be false or untrue or if any material particular is suppressed" make clear that power of termination can be exercised only if, after due inquiry in conformity with natural justice, such a finding is arrived at and not otherwise.[1]

1. Reserve Bank of India Vs C.S. Sathya Kumari 1993(2) Bank CLR 585 (Kant)

# PART II

This part consists of model Regulations; The first is Conduct Regulation and the second is Discipline and Appeal Regulations. These Regulations are made in exercise of powers under Section 19 of the Banking Companies (Acquisition and Transfer of Undertaking) Act, 1970 (5 of 1970). These Regulations are firstly approved by Ministry of Finance, Government of India and then they are made applicable to a particular Bank.

Barring small changes, these Regulations are on the same pattern in nationalised banks.

# INDEX

## OFFICER EMPLOYEES' (CONDUCT) REGULATION, 1976

# 1. MODEL OFFICER EMPLOYEES' CONDUCT REGULATIONS

## ABC BANK OF INDIA OFFICER EMPLOYEES (CONDUCT) REGULATIONS, 1976

In exercise of the powers confered by Section 10 of the Banking Companies (Acquisition and Transfer of Undertakings) Act, 1970 (5 of 1970), the Board of Director of ABC Bank of India in consultation with the Reserve Bank and with the previous sanction of the Central Government hereby makes the following regulations, namely:

## SHORT TITLE COMMENCEMENT AND APPLICATION

1. (1) These regulations may be called ABC Bank of India Officer Employees' (Conduct) Regulations, 1976.

(2) They shall come into force on 1.1.1977.

(3) They shall apply to all officer employees of the bank, recruited in India whether working in India or outside but shall not apply to—

(i) The Chairman of the bank;

(ii) The Managing Director of the Bank;

(iii) Any Whole-time Director, if any;

(iv) Those who are in casual employment or paid from the contingencies;

(v) Award Staff;

## DEFINITIONS

2. In these regulations unless the context otherwise requires—

(a) "Act" means the Banking Companies (Acquisition and Transfer of Undertakings) Act, 1970 (5 of 1970);

(b) "Award staff" means the persons covered by the "award" as defined in the Industrial Dispute (Banking Companies) Decisions Act, 1955 (41 of 1955);

(c) "Bank" mean ABC Bank of India;

(d) "Board" means the Board of Directors of the bank;

(e) "Competent authority" means the authority appointed by the Board for the purposes of these regulations;

(f) "Family" means:

(i) in the case of male officer employee, his wife, whether residing with him or not, but does not include a legally separated wife and in the case of woman officer employee her husband, whether residing with her or not, but does not include a legally separated husband;

(ii) Children or step-children of the officer employee, whether residing with the officer employee or not, wholly dependent on such officer employee but does not include children or step-children of whose custody the officer employee has been deprived of by or under any law; and

(iii) any other person related to, by blood or marriage, to the officer employee or to his spouse and wholly dependent upon such officer employee.

(g) "Government" means the Central Government;

(h) "Managing Director" means the Managing Director of the Bank;

(i) "Officer employee" means a person who holds a supervisory, administrative or managerial post in the bank or any other person who has been appointed and is functioning as an officer of the bank, by whatever designation called and includes a person whose services are temporarily placed at the disposal of the Central Government or a State Goveernment or any other Government undertaking or any other Public Sector Bank or the Reserve Bank of India or any other organisation, but shall not include casual, work charged or contingent staff or the award staff.

(j) "Public Sector Bank" means—

(i) a corresponding new bank specified in the first schedule to the Act;

(ii) a corresponding new bank specified in the First Schedule to the Banking Companies (Acquisition and Transfer of Undertakings) Act, 1980;

(iii) the State Bank of India constituted under the State Bank of India Act, 1955 (23 of 1955);

(v) a Subsidiary Bank constituted under the State Bank of India (Subsidiary Banks) Act, 1959 (38 of 1959);

(v) any other bank which the Central Government may determine to be a public sector for the purpose of these regulations, having regard to its manner of incorporation.

## GENERAL

3. (1) Every officer employee shall, at all times take all possible steps to ensure and protect the interests of the bank and discharge his duties with utmost integrity, honesty, devotion and diligence and do nothing which is unbecoming of a bank officer.

(2) Every officer employee shall maintain good conduct and discipline and show courtesy and attention to all persons in all transactions and negotiations.

(3) No officer employee shall, in the performance of his official duties or in the exercise of powers conferrned on him, act otherwise than in his best judgement except when he is acting under the direction of his official superior.

(4) Every officer employee shall take all possible steps to ensure the integrity and devotion to duty of all persons for the time being under his control and authority.

## OBSERVANCE OF SECRECY

4. Every officer employee shall maintain the strictest secrecy regarding the bank's affairs and the affairs of its constitutents and shall not divulge directly or indirectly any information of a confidential nature either to a member of the public or to an outside agency or to any other employee of the bank not entitled to such information unless—

   (i) divulging of such information is in accordance with the law or in accordance with the practices and usages customary amongst banks;

   (ii) he is compelled to divulge such information by judicial or other authority;

   (iii) instructed to do so by a superior officer in the discharge of his duties.

## EMPLOYMENT OF MEMBERS OF FAMILY OF BANK OFFICERS IN FIRMS ENJOYING THE BANK'S CLIENTAGE AND GRANT OF FACILITIES TO SUCH CONCERNS

5. (1) No officer employee shall use his position or influence directly or indirectly to secure employment for any person related, whether by blood or marriage to the employee or to the employee's wife or husband, whether such a person is dependent on the employee or not;

   (2) No officer employee shall, except with the prior permission of the competent authority permit his son, daughter or any other member of his family to accept employment in any private undertaking with which he has official dealings or in any other undertaking having to his knowedge official dealings with the bank;

   Provided that where the acceptance of the employment cannot await prior permission of the competent authority or is otherwise considered urgent, the matter shall be reported to the competent authority within three months from the date of receipt of offer of employment.

   (3) No officer employee shall, in the discharge of his official duties, knowingly grant or authorise the grant of any advance or banking facilities to or enter into or authorise entering into by or on behalf of the bank any contract, agreement, arrangement or proposal in any matter or give or sanction any contract or loan to any undertaking or person if any member of his family is employed in that undertaking or under that person or if he or any member of his family has interests in such matters or contracts in any other manner and the officer employee shall refer every such matter or contract or loan to his superior officer and the matter or contract or loan shall thereafter be disposed of according to the instructions of the authority to whom such reference is made.

   **Explanation:** A person is not deemed to have any interest in any undertaking for the purpose of this sub-regulation, if he is only a shareholder having not more than 2 per cent of the paid-up capital of the undertaking in his name.

## TAKING UP OUTSIDE EMPLOYMENT

6. (1) No officer empoyee shall, except with the previous sanction of the bank, engage directly or indirecty in any trade or business or undertake any other employment:

Provided that an officer employee may, without such sanction, undertake honorary work of a social or charitable nature or occasional work of a literary, artistic, scientific, professional, cultural, educational, religious or socal character, subject to the condition that his official duties do not thereby suffer, but he shall not undertake, or shall discontinue such work if so directed by the competent authority.

**Explanation:** Canvassing by an officer employee in support of the business of insurance agency or commission agency, owned or managed by a member of his family shall be deemed to be a breach of this sub-regulation.

(2) Every officer employee shall report to the bank if any member of his family is engaged in a trade or business or owns or manages an insurance agency or commission agency.

(3) No officer employee shall without the previous sanction of the bank except in the discharge of his official duties, take part in the registration, promotion or management of any bank or other company which is required to be registered under Companies Act, 1956 (1 of 1956) or any other law for the time being in force or any cooperative society for commercial purposes.

Provided that an officer employee may take part in registration, promotion or management of a cooperative society registered under the Co-operative Societies Act, 1912 (2 of 1912) or any other law for the time being in force, or of a literary, scientific or charitable society registered under the Societies Registration Act, 1860 (21 of 1860) or any corresponding law in force.

(4) No officer employee shall accept any fee for any work done by him for any public body or any private person without the sanction of the competent authority.

(5) No officer employee shall act as an agent of, or canvass business in favour or, an Insurance Company or Corporations in his individual capacity.

## CONTRIBUTION TO NEWSPAPERS, RADIO, ETC.

7. (1) No officer employee shall, except with the previous sanction of the competent authority, own wholly or in part or conduct or participate in the editing or management of any newspaper or any other periodical publication.

(2) No officer employee shall, except with the previous sanction of the competent authority or except in the bonafide discharge of his duties participate in radio broadcast or contribute any article or write any letter either in his own name or anonymously or in the name of any other person to any newspaper or periodical or make public, or publish or cause to be

published or pass on to others any document, paper or information which may come into his possession in his official capacity.

(3) No offficer employee shall, except with the previous sanction of the competent authority publish or cause to be published any book or any similar printed matter of which he is the author or not deliver talk or lecture in public meetings or otherwise.

Provided that no such sanction is, however, required if such broadcast or contribution or publication is of a purely literary, artistic, professional cultural, educational, religious or social character.

## DEMONSTRATIONS

8. No officer employee shall engage himself or participate in any demonstration which is prejudicial to the interests of the sovereignty and integrity of India, the security of the State, friendly relations with foreign state, public order, decency or morality or which involves contempt of court, defamation or incitement to an offence.

## JOINING OF ASSOCIATIONS PREJUDICIAL TO INTERESTS OF THE COUNTRY

9. No officer employee shall join, or continue to be a member of an association, the objects or activities of which are prejudicial to the interests the sovereignty and integrity of India or public order or morality.

## GIVING EVIDENCE

10. (1) Same as provided in sub-regulation (3), no officer employee shall, except with the previous approval of the competent authority, give evidence in connection with any equity conducted by any person, committee or authority.

(2) Where any approval has been accorded under sub-regulation (1), no officer employee giving such evidence shall criticise the policy or any action of the Government or of a State Government or of the bank.

(3) Nothing in this regulation shall apply to any evidence given—

(a) at an enquiry before an authority appointed by the Government, State Government, Parliament or a State Legislature; or

(b) in any judicial enquiry; or

(c) at any departmental enquiry ordered by the competent authority.

## PUBLIC DEMONSTRATIONS IN HONOUR OF BANK OFFICERS

11. (1) No officer employee shall, except with the previous sanction of the competent authority, receive any complementory or valedictory address or accept any testimonial or attend any meeting or entertainment held in his honour, or in the honour of any other employee of the bank.

(a) a farewell entertainment of substantially private and informal character held in honour of the officer employee or any other employee of the bank on the occasion of his retirement or transfer or any person who has recently qualified the service of the bank; and

(b) the acceptance of simple and inexpensive entertainment arranged by association of employees of the bank.

2. (a) No officer employee shall either directly or indirectly exercise pressure or influence on any employee of the bank to induce or compel him to subscribe towards any farewell entertainment.

(b) No officer employee shall collect subscription for farewell entertainment from any intermediate or lower grade employee for the entertainment of any employee belonging to any higher grade.

## SEEKING TO INFLUENCE

12. No officer employee shall bring or attempt to bring any political or other outside influence to bear upon any superior authority to further his interests in respect of matters pertaining to his service under the bank.

## ABSENCE FROM DUTY

13. (1) No officer employee shall absent himself from his duty or be late in attending office or leave the station without having first obtained the permission of the competent authority:

Provided that in the case of unavoidable circumstances where availing of prior permission is not possible or is difficult, such permission may be obtained later subject to the satisfafction of the competent authority that such a permission could not have been obtained.

(2) No officer employee shall ordinarily absent himself in case of sickness or accident without submitting a proper medical certificate:

Provided that in the case of temporary indisposition or sickness of a casual nature, the production of a medical certificate may, at the absolute discretion of the competent authority, be dispensed with.

## ACCEPTANCE OF GIFTS

14. (1) Same as otherwise provided in these regulations, no officer employee shall accept or permit any member of his family or any person acting on his behalf to accept any gift.

**Explanation:** The expression "gift" shall include free transport, boarding, lodging or other service or any other pecuniary advantage when provided by any person other than a near relative or a personal friend having no official dealings with the officer employee.

**Note:** A casual meat, lift or other social hospitability shall not be deemed to be a gift.

(2) On occasions such as marriages, anniversaries, funerals or religious functions when the making of gifts is in conformity with the prevailing religious or social practice, an officer employee may accept gifts from his near relatives but he shall make a report to the competent authority if the value of the gifts exceeds ₹ 500.

(3) On such occasions as specified in sub-regulation (2), an officer employee may also accept gifts from his personal friends having no official dealings with him but he shall make a report to the competent authority if the value of such gifts exceeds ₹ 200.

(4) In any other case, the officer employee shall not accept any gifts without the sanction of the competent authority if the value of the gifts exceeds ₹ 75.

Provided that when more than one gift has been received the matter shall be reported to the competent authority if the aggregate value thereof exceeds ₹ 500.

**Note:** As a normal practice, an officer employee shall not accept any gift from any person or institution having official dealings with the officer employee.

(5) No officer employee shall:

(i) give or take or abet the giving or taking of dowry; or

(ii) demand, directly or indirectly, from the parents or guardian of a bride or bridegroom; as the case may be, any dowry.

**Explanation:** For the purpose of this, 'dowry' has the same meaning as in the Dowry Prohibition Act, 1961 (28 of 1961).

## LENDINGS AND BORROWINGS

15. No officer shall, in his individual capacity—

(i) borrow or permit any member of his family to borrow or otherwise place himself or a member of his family under a pecuniary obligation to a broker or a money, lender or a subordinate employee of the bank or any person, association or persons, firms, company or institution, whether incorprated or not, having dealings with the bank;

(ii) buy or sell stock, shares or securities of any description without funds to meet the full cosr in the case of a purchase of scrips or delivery in the case of a sale;

(iii) incur debts at a race meeting;

(iv) lend money in private capacity to a constituent of the bank or have personal dealings with such constituent in the purchase or sale of bills of exchang, Government paper or any other securities; and

(v) guarantee in his private capacity the pecuniary obligations of another person or agree to indemnity in such capacity another person from loss except with the previous permission of the competent authority.

Provided that an officer employee may, give to or accept from a relative or personal friend a purely temporary loan of a small amount free of interest, or operate a credit account with a bonafide tradesman or make an advance of pay to his private employee.

Provided further that an officer employee may obtain a loan from a cooperative credit society of which he is a member or stand as a surety in respect of a loan taken by another member from a cooperative credit society of which he is a member.

## ADVANCE DRAWAL OF SALARY

16. No officer employee shall draw his salary in advance or overdraw his account with the bank against security or otherwise without the previous sanction of the competent authority.

## SUBSCRIPTIONS

17. No other employee shall, except with the previous sanction of the competent authority, ask for or accept contributions to or otherwise associate himself with the raising of any funds or other collections in cash or in kind in pursuance of any objective whatsoever.

## SPECULATIONS IN STOCKS AND SHARES AND INVESTMENTS

18. No officer employee shall speculate in any stock, share or securities or commodities or valuables of any descriptions or shall make investments which are likely to embarrass or influence him in the discharge of his duties:

Provided that nothing in this regulation shall be deemed to prohibit an officer employee from making a bonafide investment of his own funds in such securities as he may wish to buy.

**Note:** Frequent purchase or sale or both of shares or securities or other investments shall be deemed to be speculation for the purpose of this regulation.

## INDEBTEDNESS

19. An officer employee shall so manage his private affairs as to avoid habitual indebtedness or insolvency. An officer employee against whom any legal proceedings are instituted for the recovery of any debt due from him or for adjudging him as an insolvent shall fortwith report the full facts of the legal proceedings to the bank.

## MOVABLE, IMMOVABLE AND VALUABLE PROPERTY

20. (1) Every officer employee, on his first appointment, and every other employee of the bank, on promotion to a post of an officer employee in the bank, shall submit a return of his assets and liabilities giving full particulars regarding:

(a) the immovable property inherited by him or owned or acquired by him or held by him on lease or mortgage, either in his name or in the name of any member of his family or in the name of any other person;

(b) shares, debentures and cash including bank deposits inherited by him or similarly owned or acquired or held by him;

(c) other movable property inherited by him or similarly owned or acquired or held by him; and

(d) debts and other liabilities incurred by him directly or indrectly:

Provided that in the case of an officer employee who is already in service in the bank on the date these regulations come into force, shall submit a return in terms of this regulation within three months of coming into force of these regulations, the return being with reference to the assets and liabilities as enumerated above of the officer employee on the date these regulations come into force.

(2) Every officer employee shall, every year submit a return of his movable, immovable and valuable property including liquid assets like shares, debentures, as on 31st March of that year, to the bank before the 30th day of June of that year.

(3) No officer employee shall except with the previous knowledge of the competent authority acquire or dispose of any immovable property by lease, mortgage, purchase, sale, gift or otherwise either in his own name or in the name of any member of his family:

Provided that the previous saction of the competent authority shall be obtained by the officer employee if any such transaction is:

(a) with a person having official dealings with the employee; or

(b) otherwise than through a regular or reputed dealer;

(4) Every officer employee shall report to the competent authority every transaction concerning movable property owned or held by him either in his own name or in the name of a member of his family if the value of such a property exceeds ₹ 5,000/-.

Provided that the previous sacntion of the competent authority shall be obtained if any such transaction is:

(a) with a person having official dealings with the officer employee; or

(b) otherwise than through a regular or reputed dealer.

(i) The term every transaction concerning movable property referred to in Regulation 20(4) shall include all transactions of sale or of purchase.

(ii) For the purpose of this sub-regulation, the definition of movable property would include:

(a) Jewellery, insurance policies, the annual premia of which exceeds ₹ 2,500/- or one-sixth of the total annual emoluments received from the Bank, whichever is less, shares, securities and debentures;

(b) Loans advanced by such employee whether secured or not;

(c) Motor Cars, Motor Cycles, Horses or any other means of conveyance; and

(d) refrigerators, radios (radiograms and television sets), etc.

(iii) Transactions entered into by the spouse or any other member of family of an Officer employee of the Bank out of his or her own funds (including stridhan, gifts, inheritance, etc.) as distinct from the funds of the Officer employee of the Bank himself/herself in his or her own name and in his or her own right, would not attract the above provisions.

(5) The bank may at any time, by general or special order, require an officer employee to furnish within a period to be specified in the order a full and complete statement of such movable or immovable property held or acquired by him or on his behalf or by any member of his family as may be specified in the order. Such a statement shall, if so required by the bank, include the details of the means by which or the sources from such property was acquired.

## VINDICATION OF ACTS AND CHARACTER OF OFFICER EMPLOYEE

21. No offficer employee shall, except with the previous sanction of the bank, have recourse to any court or to the press for the vindication of any official act which has been the subject-matter of adverse criticism or an attack of a defamatory character:

Provided that nothing in this regulation shall be deemed to prohibit an employee from vindcating his private character or any act done by him in his private capacity and where any action for vindicating his private character or any act done by him in private capacity is taken, the officer employee shall submit a report to his immediate within a period of three months from the date such action is taken by him.

## RESTRICTIONS REGARDING MARRIAGE

22. (1) (i) No officer employee shall enter into, or contract, a marriage with a person having a spouse living and

(ii) No officer employee, having a spouse living, shall enter into, or contract, a marriage with any person:

Provided that the bank may permit an officer employee to enter into, or contract, any such marriage as is referred in clause (i) or clause (ii) if it is satisfied that—

(a) such marriage is permisiable under the personal law applicante to such officer employee and the other party to the marriage, and

(b) there are other grounds for so doing.

(2) An officer employee who has married or marries a person other than of Indian Nationality shall forthwith intimates the fact to the bank.

## CONSUMPTION OF INTOXICATING DRINKING AND DRUGS

23. An Officer employee shall:

(a) strictly abide by any law relating to intoxicating drinks or drugs in force in any area in which he may happen to be for the time being;

(b) not be under the influence of any intoxicating drink or drug during the course of his duty and shall also take due care that the performance of his duties at any time is not affected in any way by the influence of such drink or drug;

(c) refrain from consuming any intoxicating drink or drug in a public place;

(d) not appear in a public place in a state of intoxication;

(e) not use any intoxicating drink or drug to excess.

**Explanation:** For the purpose of this rule, 'public place' means any place or premises (including clubs, even exclusively meant for members where it is permissible for the members to invite non-members as guests, bars and restaurants, conveyance) to which the public have or are permitted to have access, whether on payment or otherwise.

## ACTS OF MISCONDUCT

24. A breach of any of the provisions of these regulations shall be deemed to constitute a misconduct punishable under the Central Bank of India Officer Employees' (Discipline and Appeal) Regulations, 1976.

## INTERPRETATION

25. If any question arises as to the application or interpretation of any of these regulations, it shall be referred to the Board for its decision.

## REPEAL AND SAVING

26. (1) Every rule, regulation, bye-law or every provision in any agreement or resolution corresponding to any of the regulations herein contained and in force immediately before the commencement of these regulations and applicable is hereby repealed;

(2) Notwithstanding such repeal any order made or action taken under the provisions so repealed shall be deemed to be made or taken under the corresponding provisions of these regulations.

# INDEX

## ABC BANK OF INDIA OFFICER EMPLOYEES' (DISCIPLINE AND APPEAL) REGULATONS, 1976

# 2. MODEL OFFICER EMPLOYEE'S DISCIPLINE AND APPEAL REGULATIONS

# ABC BANK OF INDIA OFFICER EMPLOYEES' (DISCIPLINE AND APPEAL) REGULATIONS, 1976

In exercise of the powers conferred by Section 18 of the Banking Companies (Acquisition and Transfer of Undertakings) Act, 1970 (5 of 1970), the Board of Directors of ABC Bank of India in consultation with Reserve Bank and with the previous santion of the Central Government hereby makes the following regulations, namely:

## SHORT TITLE AND COMMENCEMENT

1. (i) These regulations may be called ABC Bank of India Officer Empoyees' (Discipline and Appeal) Regulations, 1976.

   (ii) They shall come into force on 1.1.1977.

## APPLICATION

2. There regulations shall apply to all officer employees of the Bank, but shall not apply to—

   (i) the Chairman of the Bank;

   (ii) the Managing Director;

   (iii) any Whole-time Director, if any;

   (iv) those who are in casual employment or paid from contingencies;

   (v) the Award Staff; an

   (vi) the officers on contract.

## DEFINITIONS

3. In these regulations unless the context otherwise requires—

   (a) "Act" means the Banking Companies (Acquisition and Transfer of Undertakings) Act, 1970 (5 of 1970);

   (b) "Appellate Authority" means the authority specified in the Schedule to dispose of appeals;

   (c) "Award staff" means the persons covered by the "award" as defined in the Industrial Disputes (Banking Companies) Decision Act, 1955 (41 of 1955);

   (d) "Bank" mean ABC Bank of India;

   (e) "Board" means the Board of Directors of the Bank;

   (f) "Competent Authority" means the authority appointed by the Board for the purposes of these regulations;

(g) "Disciplinary Authority" means the authority specified in the Schedule which is competent to impose on an Officer employee any of the penalties specified in Regulation 4;

(h) "Government" means the Central Government;

(i) "Managing Director" means the Managing Director of the Bank;

(j) "Official employee" means a person who holds a supervisory, administrative or managerial post in the bank of any other person who has appointed and is functioning as an officer of the bank, by whatever designations called and includes a person whose services are temporarily placed at the disposal of the Central Government or a State Government or any other Government undertaking or any other Public Sector Bank of the Reserve Bank of India or any other organisation, but shall not include casual, work charged or contingent staff or the award staff;

(k) "public financial institutions" means—

(i) the Industrial Credit and Investment Corporation of India Limited, a company owned and registered under the Companies Act, 1956 (1 of 1956);

(ii) the Industrial Finance Corporation of India, established under Section 3 of the Industrial Finance Corporation Act, 1948 (15 of 1948);

(iii) the Industrial Development Bank of India established under Section 3 of the Industrial Development Bank of India Act, 1964 (18 of 1964);

(iv) the Life Insurance Corporation of India established under Section 3 of the Life Insurance Corporation Act, 1965 (31of 1966);

(v) the Unit Trust of India, established under Section 3 of the Unit Trust of India Act, 1963 (52 of 1963);

(vi) any officer financial institution which is declared by the Central Government by notification to be a public financial institution;

(l) "Public Sector Banks" means—

(i) a corresponding new bank specified in the first schedule to the act;

(ii) a corresponding new bank specified in the First Schedule to the Banking Companies (Acquisition and Transfer of Undertakings) Act, 1980;

(iii) the State Bank of India constituted under the State Bank of India Act, 1955 (23 of 1955);

(iv) a subsidiary bank constituted under the State Bank of India (Subsidiary Banks) Act, 1959 (38 of 1959); and

(v) any other bank which the Central Government may determine to be a public sector bank for the purpose of these regulations having regard to its manner of incorporation;

(m) "Public servant" means a person defined as public servant in Section 21 of the Indian Penal Code (45 of 1860);

(n) "Reviewing Authority" means the authority specified in schedule;

(o) "Schedule" means the Schedule appended to these regulations.

## PENALTIES

4. The following are the penalties which may be imposed on an officer employee, for acts of misconduct or for any other good and sufficient reasons.

**Minor Penalties**

(a) Censure;

(b) Withholding of incrementals of pay with or without cumulative effect;

(c) Withholding of promotion;

(d) Recovery from pay of such other amount as may be due to him of the whole or part of any pecuniary loss caused to the Bank by negligence or breach of orders;

(e) Reduction to a lower stage in the time scale of pay for a period not exceeding 3 years, without cumulative effect and not adversely affecting the Officer's pension.

**Major Penalties:**

(f) Same as provided for in (e) above reduction to a lower stage in the time scale of pay for a specified period, with further directions as to whether or not the officer will earn increments of pay during the period of such reduction and whether on the expiry of such period the reduction will or will not have the effect of postponing the future increments of his pay;

(g) Reduction to a lower grade or post;

(h) Compulsory retirement;

(i) Removal from service which shall not be a disqualification for future employment;

(j) Dismissal which shall ordinarily be a disqualification for future employment.

**Explanation:** The following shall not amount to a penalty within the meaning of this regulation namely:

(i) withholding of one or more increments of an officer employee on account of his failure to pass a prescribed departmental test or examination in accordance with the terms of appointment to the post which he holds;

(ii) stoppage of pay of an officer employee at the efficiency bar in a time scale, on the ground of his unfitness to cross the bar;

(iii) non-promotion, whether in an offiiciating capacity or otherwise, of an officer employee, to a higher grade or post for which he may be eligible for consideration but for which he is found unsuitable after consideration of his case;

(iv) reversion to a lower grade or post, of an officer employee officiating in a higher grade or post, on the ground that he is considered, after trial, to be unsuitable for such higher grade or post, or on administrative grounds, unconnected with his conduct;

(v) reversion to his previous grade or post, of an officer employee appointed on a probation to another grade or post, during or at the end of the period of probation, in accordance with the terms of his appointment or rules or orders governing such probation;

(vi) reversion of an officer employee to his parent organisation in case he had come on deputation;

(vii) termination of the service:

(a) of an officer employee appointed on probation, during or at the end of the period of probation, in accordance with the terms of his appointment, or the rules or orders governing such probation;

(b) of an officer employee appointed in a temporary capacity otherwise than under a contract or agreement, on the expiration of the period for which he was appointed, or earlier in accordance with the terms of his appointment;

(c) of an officer employee appointed under a contract or agreement, in accordance with the terms of such contract or agreement; and

(d) of an officer employee on abolition of post;

(viii) retirement of an officer employment on his attaining the age of superannuation in accordance with the rules and orders governing such superannuation;

(ix) termination of employment of a permanent officer employee by giving 3 months' notice or on payment of 3 months' pay and allowances in lieu of notice;

(x) termination of employment of an officer employee on medical grounds, if he is declared unfit to continue in bank's service by the Bank's medical officer.

## AUTHORITY TO INSTITUTE DISCIPLINARY PROCEEDINGS AND IMPOSE PENALTIES

5. (1) The Managing Director or any other authority empowered by him by general or special order may institute or direct the Disciplinary Authority to institute disciplinary proceedings against an officer employee of the Bank.

(2) The Disciplinary Authority may himself institute disciplinary proceedings.

(3) The Disciplinary Authority or any authority higher than it, may impose any of the penalties specified in Regulation 4 on any officer employee.

## PROCEDURE FOR IMPOSING MAJOR PENALTIES

6. (1) No order imposing any of the major penalties specified in Clauses (f), (g), (h), (i) and (j) of Regulation 4 shall be made except after an enquiry is held in accordance with this Regulation.

(2) Whenever the Disciplinary Authority is of the opinion that there are grounds for inquiring into the truth of any imputation of misconduct or misbehaviour against an officer employee, it may itself inquire into, or appoint any other public servant (hereinafter referred to as the Inquiring Authority) to inquire into the thereof.

**Explanation:** When the Disciplinary Authority itself holds the inquiry any reference in sub-regulation (8) to sub-regulation (2) to the Inquiring Authority shall be construed as a reference to Disciplinary Authority.

(3) Where it is proposed to hold an inquiry, the Dsciplinary Auhority shall frame definite and distinct charges on the basis of the allegations against the officer employee and the articles of charge, together with a statement of the allegations, on which they are based, shall be cmmunicated in writing to the officer employee, who shall be required to submit within such time as may be specified by the Disciplinary Authority (not exceeding 15 days), or within such extended time as may be granted by the said Authority, a written statement of his defence.

(4) On receipt of the written statement of the officer employee, or if no such statement is received within the time specified, an inquiry may be held by the Disciplinary Authority itself, or if it considers it necessary so to appoint under sub-regulation (2) an Inquiring Authority for the purpose:

Provided that it may not be necessary to hold an inquiry in respect of the articles of change admitted by the officer employee in his written statement but shall be necessary to record its findings on each such change.

(5) The Disciplinary Authority shall, where it is not the inquiring authority, forward to the Inquiring Authority):

(i) a copy of the articles of charges and statements of imputations of misconduct or misbehaviour;

(ii) a copy of the written statement of defence, if any submitted by the officer employee;

(iii) a list of documents by which and list of witnesses by whom the articles of charge are proposed to be substantiated;

(iv) a copy of statements of the witnesses, if any;

(v) evidence proving the delivery of articles of charge under sub-regulation (3);

(vi) a copy of the order appointing the 'Presenting Officer' in terms of sub-regulation (6).

(6) Where the Disciplinary Authority itself inquiries or appoints an inquiring authority for holding an inquiry, it may, by an order, appoint a public servant to be known as the "Presenting Officer" to present on its behalf the case in support of the articles of charge.

(7) The Officer employee may take the assistance of any other Officer employee but may not engage a legal practitioner for the purpose, unless the Presenting Officer appointed by the Disciplinary Authority is a legal practitioner or the Disciplinary Authority having regard to the circumstances of the case so permits.

**Note:** The Officer employee shall not take the assistance of any other Officer employee who has two pending disciplinary cases on hand in which he has to give assistance.

(8) (a) The Inquiring Authority shall by notice in writing specify the day on which the officer employee shall appear in person before the Inquiring Authority.

(b) On the date fixed by the Inquiring Authority, the officer employee shall appear before the Inquiring Authority at the time, place and date specified in the notice.

(c) The Inquiring Authority shall ask the officer employee whether he pleads guilty or has any defence to make and if he pleads guilty to any of the articles of change, the Inquiring Authority shall record the plea, sign the record and obtain the signature of the officer employee concerned thereon.

(d) The Inquiring Authority shall return a finding of guilt in respect of those articles of charge to which the officer employee concerned pleads guilty.

(9) If the officr employee dos not plead guilty, the Inquiring Authority shall adjourn the case to a later date not exceeding 30 days or within such extended time as may be granted by the Inquiring Authority.

(10) (a) The Inquiring Authority shall, where the officer employee does not admit all or any of the articles of charge, furnish to such officer employee a list of documents by which, and a list witnesses by whom, the articles of change are proposed to be proved.

(b) The Inquiring Authority shall also record an order that the officer employee may for the purpose of preparing his defence:

(i) inspect within five days of the order or within such further time not exceeding five days as the Inquiring Authority may allow, the documents listed;

(ii) submit a list of documents and witnesses that he wants for the inquiry;

(iii) be supplied with copies of statements of witnesses, if any, recorded earlier and the Inquiring Authority shall furnish such copies not later than three days before the commencement of the examination of the witnesses by the Inquiring Authority;

(iv) give a notice within ten days of the order or within such further time not exceedig ten days as the Inquiring Authority may allow for the discovery of production of the documents referred to in item (ii).

**Note:** The relevancy of the documents and the examination of the witnesses referred to in item (ii) shall be given by the officer employee concerned.

(11) The Inquiring Authority shall, on receipt of the notice for the discovery or production of the documents, forward the same or copies thereof to the authority in whose custody or possession the documents are kept with a requisition for the production of documents on such date as may be specified.

(12) On the receipt of the requisition under sub-regulation (11), the authority having the custody or possession of the requisitioned documents, shall arrange to produce the same before the Inquiring Authority on the date, place and time specified in the requisition:

Provided that the authority having the custody or possession of the requisitioned documents may claim privilege if the production of such documents will be against the public interest or the interest of the bank. In that event, it shall inform the Inquiring Authority accordingly.

(13) On the date fixed for the inquiry, the oral and documentary evidence by which the Articles of charges are proposed to be proved shall be produced by or on behalf of the Disciplinary Authority. The witnesses produced by the Presenting Officer or by another officer duly nominated by the Disciplinary Authority to act on behalf of Presenting Officer shall be examined by the Presenting Officer or by the officer nominated by the Disciplinary Authority to act on behalf of the Presenting Officer and may be cross-examined by or on behalf of the officer employee. The Presenting Officer or the officer nominated to act on his behalf shall be entitled to re-examine his witnesses on any point on which they have been cross-examined, but not on a new matter without the leave of the Inquiring Authority. The Inquiring Authority may also put such questions to the witnesses as it thinks fit.

(14) Before the close of the case, in support of the charges, the Inquiring Authority may, in its discretion, allow the Presenting Officer to produce evidence not included in the charge-sheet or may itself call for new evidence or recall or re-examine any witness. In such case, the officer employee shall be given opportunity to inspect the documentary evidence before it is taken on record or to cross-examine a witness who has been so summoned. The Inquiring

Officer may also allow the officer employee to produce new evidence, if it is of opinion that the production of such evidence is necessary in the interests of justice.

(15) When the case in support of the charges is closed, the officer employee may be required to state his defence, orally or in writing as he may prefer. If the defence is made orally, it shall be recorded and the officer employee shall be required to sign the recrd. In either case, a copy of the statement of defence shall be given to the Presenting Officer, if any, appointed.

(16) The evidence on behalf of the officer employee shall then be produced. The officer employee may examine in his own behalf, if he so prefers. The witnesses produced by the officer employee shall then be examined by the officer employee and may be cross-examined by the Presenting Officer. The officer employee shall be entitled to re-examine any of his witnesses on any points on which they have been cross-examined, but not on any new matter without the leave of the Inquiring Authority.

(17) The Inquiring Autority may, after the office employee closes his evidence, and shall, if the officer employee has not got himself examined, generally question him on the circumstances appearing against him in the evidence for the purpose of enabling the officer employee explain any circumstances appearing in the evidence against him.

(18) The Inquiring Authority may, after the completion of the production of evidence, hear the Presenting Officer, if any appointed and the Officer Employee, or permit them to file written briefs of their respective case within 15 days of the date of completion of the production of evidence if they so desire.

(19) If the officer employee does not submit the written statement of defence referred to in sub-regulation (3) on or before the date specified for the purpose or does not appear in person, or through the assisting officer or otherwise fails or refuses to comply with any of the provisions of these regulations, the Inquiring Authority may hold the inquiry ex-parte.

(20) Whenever any Inquiring Authority, after having heard and recorded the whole or any part of the evidence in an inquiry ceases to exercise jurisdiction therein, and is succeeded by another Inquiring Authority which has, and which exercises, such jurisdiction, the Inquiring Authority so suceeding may act on the evidence so recorded by its predecessor, or partly recorded by its predecessor and partly recorded by itself:

Provided that if the suceeding Inquiring Authority is of the opinion that further examination of any of the witnesses whose evidence has already been recorded is necessary in the interest of justice, it may recall, examine, cross-examine and re-examine any such witnesses as herein before provided.

(21) (i) On the conclusion of the inquiry, the Inquiring Authority shall prepare a report which shall contain the following:

(a) a gist of the articles of change and the statement of the imputation of misconduct or misbehaviour;

(b) a gist of the defence of the officer employee in respect of each article of charge;

(c) an assessment of the evidence in respect of each article of charge;

(d) the findings on each article of charge and the reasons therefor.

**Explanation:** If, in the opinion of the Inquiring Authority, the proceedings of the inquiry establish any article of charge different from the original article of charge, it may record its findings on such article of charge.

Provided that the findings on such article of charge shall not be recorded unless the officer employee has either admitted the facts on which such article of charge is based or has had a reasonable opportunity of defending himself against article of charge.

(ii) The Inquiring Authority, where it is not itself the Disciplinary Authority, shall forward to the Disciplinary Authority the records of inquiry which shall include:

(a) the report of the inquiry prepared by it under clause (i);

(b) the written statement of defence, if any, submitted by the officer employee referred to in sub-regulation (15);

(c) the oral and documentary evidence produced in the course of the inquiry;

(d) written briefs referred to in sub-regulation (18), if any; and

(e) the orders, if any, made by the Disciplinary Authority and the Inquiring Authority in regard to the inquiry.

## ACTION ON THE INQUIRY REPORT

7. (1) The Disciplinary Authority, if it is not itself the Inquiring Authority, may, for reasons to be recorded by it in writing, remit the case to the Inquiring Authority for fresh or further inquiry and report and the Inquiring Authority shall thereupon proceed to hold the further inquiry according to the provisions of Regulation 6 as far as may be.

(2) The Disciplinary Authority shall, if it disagrees with the findings of Inquiring Authority on any article of charge, record its reasons for such disagreement and record its own findings on such charge, if the evidence on record is sufficient for the purpose.

(3) If the Diciplinary Authority, having regard to its findings on all or any of the articles of change, is of the opinion that any of the penalties specified in Regulation 4 should be imposed on the officer employee it

shall, notwithstanding anything contained in Regulation 8, make an order imposing such penalty.

(4) If the Disciplinary Authority having regard to its findings on all or any of the articles of charge, is of the opinion that no penalty is called for, it may pass an order exonerating the officer employee concerned.

## PROCEDURE FOR IMPOSING MINOR PENALTIES

8. (1) Where it is proposed to impose any of the minor penalties specified in Clauses (a) to (e) of Regulation 4, the Officer employee concerned shall be informed in writing of the imputations of lapses against him and give an opportunity to submit his written statement of defence within a specified period not exceeding 15 days or such extended period as may be granted by the Disciplinary Authority and the defence statement if any, submitted by the Officer employee shall be taken into consideration by the Disciplinary Authority before passing orders.

(2) Where, however, the Disciplinary Authority is satisfied that an inquiry is necessary, it shall follow the procedure for imposing a major penalty as laid down in Regulation 6.

(3) The record of the proceedings in such cases shall include:

(i) a copy of the statement of imputations of lapses furnished to the officer employee;

(ii) the defence statement, if any, of the officer employee; and

(iii) the orders of the Disciplinary Authority together with the reasons therefor.

## COMMUNICATION OF ORDERS

9. Orders made by the Disciplinary Authority under Regulation 7 or Regulation 8 shall be communicated to the officer employee concerned, who shall also be supplied with a copy of the report of inquiry, if any.

## COMMON PROCEEDINGS

10. Where two or more officer employees are concerned in a case, the authority competent to impose a major penalty on all such officer employees may make an order directing that disciplinary proceedings against all of them may be taken in a common proceeding.

## SPECIAL PROCEDURE IN CERTAIN CASES

11. Notwithstanding anything contained in Regulation 6 or Regulation 8, the Disciplinary Authority may impose any of the penalties specified in Regulation 4 if the officer employee has been convicted on a criminal charge, or on the strength of facts or conclusions arrive at by a judicial trial:

Provided that the officer employee may be given an opportunity of making representation on the penalty proposed to be imposed before any order is made.

## SUSPENSION

12. (1) An officer employee may be placed under suspension by the competent authority—

(a) where a disciplinary proceeding against him is contemplated or is pending; or

(b) where a case against him in respect of any criminal offence is under investigation, inquiry or trial.

(2) An officer employee shall be deemed to have been placed under suspension by an order of the competent authority—

(a) with effect frrom the date of his detention, if he is detained in custody, whether on a criminal charge or otherwise, for a period exceeding forty-eight hours;

(b) with effect from the date of conviction, if in the event of a conviction for an offence, he is sentenced to a term of imprisonment exceeding forty-eight hours and is not forthwith dismissed or removed or compulsorily retired consequent to such conviction.

**Explanation:** The period of forty-eight hours referred to in clause (b) of this sub-regulation shall be computed from the commencement of the imprisonment after the conviction and for this purpose, intermittent periods of imprisonment, if any, shall be taken into account.

(3) Where a penalty of dismisal, removal or compulsory retirement from service imposed upon an officer employee under suspension is set aside in appeal or on review under these regulations and the case is remitted for further inquiry or action or with any directions, the order of his suspension shall be deemed to have continued in force on and from the date of the original order of dismisal, removal or compulsory retirement and shall remain in force until further orders.

(4) Where a penalty of dismisal, removal or compulsory retirement from service imposed upon an officer employee under suspension is set aside or declared or rendered void in consequence of or by a decision of a court or law, and the Disciplinary Authority, on consideration of the circumstances of the case decides to hold further inquiry against him on the allegations on which the penalty of dismissal, removal or compulsory retirement was originally imposed, the officer employe shall be deemed to have been placed under suspension by the competent authority from the date of the original order of dismissal, removal or compulsory

retirement and shall contiue to remain under suspension until further orders.

(5) (a) An order of suspension made or deemed to have been under this regulation shall continue to remain in force until it is modified or revoked by the authority competent to do so.

(b) An order of suspension made or deemed to have been made under this regulation may at any time be modified or revoked by the authority which made or is deemed to have made the order.

## LEAVE DURING SUSPENSION

13. No leave shall be granted to an officer employee under suspension.

## SUBSISTENCE ALLOWANCE DURING SUSPENSION

14. (1) An officer employee who is placed under suspension shall, during the period of such suspension and subject to sub-regulation (2) to (4) be entitled to receive payment from the bank by way of subsistence allowance on the following scale, namely:

**(a) Basic Pay:**

(i) For the first three months of suspension, 1/3 of the basic pay which the officer employee was receiving of the date prior to the date of suspension irrespective of the nature of inquiry.

(ii) For the subsequent perid after 3 months from the date of suspension:

(1) where the inquiry is held by the bank, 1/2 of the basic pay, the officer employee was drawing on the date prior to the date of suspension, and

(2) where the inquiry is held by an outside agency, 1/3 of the basic pay for the next three months and 1/2 of the basic pay for the remaining period of suspension.

**(b) Allowances:**

For the entire period of suspension, dearness allowance and other allowance excepting conveyance allowance/entertainment allowance and special allowance will be calculated on the reduced pay as specified in items (i) and (ii) of clause (a) and at the prevailing rates or at rates applicable to similar category of officers.

(2) If an officer under suspension continued to occupy the rent-free quarters provided to him by the Bank, a rent equal to ten per cent of the subsistence allowance payable to the officer may be collected as monthly rent for the premises occupied by him.

(3) No officer employee of the bank shall be entitled to receive payment of subsistence allowance unless he furnishes a certificate that he is not engaged in any other employment, business, profession or vocation.

(4) If, during the period of suspension, an officer employee retires by reason of his attaining the age of superanuation, no subsistence allowance shall be paid to him from the date of his retirement.

## PAY, ALLOWANCES AND TREATMENT OF SERVICE ON TERMINATION OF SUSPENSION

15. (1) Where the competent authority holds that the officer employee has been fully exonerated or that the suspension was unjustifiable, the officer employee concerned shall be granted the full pay to which he would have been entitled, had he not been suspended, together with any allowance of which he was in receipt immediately prior to his suspension, or may have been sanctioned subsequently and made applicable to all officer employees.

(2) In all cases other than those referred to in sub-regulation (1), the officer employee shall be granted such proportion of pay and allowances as the Competent Authority may direct:

Provided that the payment of allowances under this sub-regulation shall be subject to all other conditions to which such allowances are admissible:

Provided further that the pay and allowances granted under this sub-regulation shall not be less than the subsistence and other allowances admissible under Regulation 14.

(3) (a) In a case falling under sub-regulation (1), the period of absence from duly shall, for all purposes, be treated as a period spent on duty;

(b) In a case falling under sub-regulation (2), the period of absence from duty shall not be treated as a period spent on duty unless the Competent Authority specifically directs, for reasons to be recorded in writing, that it shall be so treated for any specific purpose.

## EMPLOYEES ON DEPUTATION FROM THE CENTRAL GOVERNMENT, STATE GOVERNMENT, ETC.

16. (1) Where an order of suspension is made or disciplinary proceedings is taken against an officer employee, who is on deputation to the bank from the Central Government or State Government, or Reserve Bank of India or another public sector bank or banking company or a public financial institution or an institution wholly or substantially owned by the Reserve Bank of India or a public financial institution or public undertaking, or a local authority, the authority lending his services (hereinafter referred to as "Lending Authoriy") shall forthwith be informed of the circumstances leading to the order of his suspension, or the commencement of the disciplinary proceedings, as the cases may be.

(2) In the light of the findings in the disciplinary proceedings taken against the officer employee:

(a) If the Disciplinary Authority is of the opinion that any of the minor penalties should be imposed on him, it may pass such orders on the case as it deems necessary after consultation with Lending Authority:

Provided that in the event of a difference of opinion between the Disciplinary Authority and the Lending Authority, the services of the employee shall be placed at the disposal of the Lending Authority.

(b) If the Disciplinary Authority is of the opinion that any of the major penalties should be imposed on him, it should replace his services at the disposal of the Lending Authority and transmit to it the proceedings of the inquiry for such action as it deems necessary.

(3) If the officer employee submits an appeal against an order imposing a minor penalty on him under clause (a) of sub-regulation (2), it will be disposed of after consultation with the Lending Authority:

Provided that if there is a difference of opinion between the Appellate Authority and the Lending Authority, the services of the officer employee shall be placed at the disposal of the Lending Authority, and the proceedings of the case shall be transmitted to that authority for such action as it deems necessary.

## APPEALS

17. (i) An officer employee may appeal against an order imposing upon him any of the penalties specified in Regulation 4 or against the order of suspension referred to in Regulation 12. The appeal shall lie to the Appellate Authority.

(ii) An appeal shall be preferred within 45 days from the date of receipt of the order appealed against. The appeal shall be addressed to the Appellate Authority and submitted to the authority whose order is appealed against. The authority whose order is appealed against shall forward the appeal together with its comments and the records of the case to the Appellate Authority. The Appellate Authority shall consider whether the findings are justified or whether the penalty is excessive or inadequate and pass appropriate orders. The Appellate Authority may pass an order confirming, enhancing, reducing or setting aside the penalty or remitting the case to the authority which imposed the penalty or to any other authority with such direction as it may deem fit in the circumstances of the case:

Provided that —

(i) If the enhanced penalty which the Appellate Authority proposed to impose a major penalty specified in Clauses (f), (g), (h), (i) and (j) of Regulation 4 and an inquiry as provided in Regulation 6 has not already been held in the case, the Appellate Authority shall direct that such an inquiry be held in accordance with the provision of Regulation 6 and thereafter consider the record of the inquiry and pass such orders as it may deem proper.

(ii) If the Appellate Authority decides to enhance the punishment but an inquiry has already been held as provided in Regulation 6, the Appellate Authority shall give a show cause notice to the officer employee as to why the enhanced penalty should not be imposed upon him and shall pass final order after taking into account the representation, if any submitted by the officer employee.

## REVIEW

18. Notwithstanding anything contained in these regulations, the Reviwing Authority may call for the record of the case within six months of the date of the final order and after reviewing the case pass such orders thereon as it may deem. it;

Provided that:

(i) If any enhanced penalty which the Reviewing Authority proposes to impose, is a major penalty specified in Clauses (f), (g), (h), (i) or (j) of Regulation 4 and an inquiry as provided under Regulation 6 has not already been held in the case, the Reviewing Authority shall direct that such an inquiry be held in accordance with the provisions of Regulaion 6 and thereafter, consider the record of the inquiry and pass such order as it may deem proper.

(ii) If the Reviewing Authority decides to enhance the punishment but an inquiry has already been held in accordance with the provisions of Regulation 6, the Reviewing Authority shall give show cause notice to the officer employees as to why the enhanced penalty should not be imposed upon him and shall pass an order after taking account the representation, if any, submitted by the officer employee.

## CONSULTATION WITH CENTRAL VIGILANCE COMMISSION

19. The bank shall consult the Central Vigilance Commission wherever necessary, in respect of all disciplinary cases having a vigilance angle.

## SERVICE OF ORDERS, NOTICE, ETC.

20. Every order, notice and other process made or issued under these regulations shall be served in person on the officer employee concerned or communicated to him by registered post at his last known address.

## POWER TO RELAX TIME-LIMIT AND TO CONDONE DELAY

21. Same as otherwise expressly provided in these regulations, the authority competent under these regulations to make any order may, for good and sufficient reasons or if sufficient cause is shown, extend the time specified in these regulations for anything required to be done these regulations or condone any delay.

## REPEAL AND SAVING

22. (1) Every rule, regulation, bye-law or every provision in any agreement or a resolution corresponding to any of the regulations herein contained and in force immediately before the commencement of these regulations and applicable to the officer employees is recently repealed.

(2) Notwithstanding such repeal—

(a) any order made or action taken under the provisions so repealed shall be deemed to have been made or taken under the corresponding provisions of these regulations;

(b) nothing in these regulations shall be construed as depriving any person to whom these regulations apply, of any right of appeal which had accrued to him under any of the provisions so repealed;

(c) an appeal pending at the commencement of these regulations against an order made before the commencement of these regulation shall be considered and orders thereon shall be made, in accordance with these regulations;

(d) any proceeding which have already been initiated but not yet been completed at the commencement of these regulations shall be continued and disposed as far as may be, in accordance with the provisions of these regulations, as if such proceedings were under these regulations.

# SCHEDULE

# ABC BANK OF INDIA OFFICER EMPLOYEES' (DISCIPLINE AND APPEAL) REGULATIONS, 1976

## DISCIPLINARY AUTHORITY

1. Any Officer of the Bank, not lower in rank and status than a Chief Manager/ Regional Manager (Scale IV), shall be competent to act as the Disciplinary Authority under these Regulations, in regard to disciplinary proceedings against any officer employee lower in rank and status than himself. PROVIDED that if such Disciplinary Authority chooses to entrust the inquiry to any other public servant, in terms of Regulation 6(2), he shall, as far as possible, entrust such inquiry to one of the Officer employees of the Bank not lower in rank and status than a Manager or Branch Manager, Medium Category or any other officer of equivalent rank.

   The Disciplinary Authority shall be competent to transfer any inquiry, at any stage, from one Inquiring Authority to another with instructions either to hold the inquiry de novo or to continue the inquiry from the stage at which it was pending with the previous Inquiring Authority.

## APPELLATE AUTHORITY

2. Any Officer employee of the Bank higher in rank and status than the Disciplinary Authority but not lower in rank and status than an Assistant General Manager shall be competent to act as the Appellate Authority within the meaning of Regulation 17.

## REVIEWING AUTHORITY

3. Any Officer employee of the Bank, not lower in rank and status, than a Deputy General Manager, shall be competent to act as the Reviewing Authority in respect of any inquiry held against an Officer employee lower in rank and status than such Reviewing Authority.

## COMPETENT AUTHORITY

4. Any Officer of the Bank, not lower in rank and status, than a Regional Manager/ Chief Manager (Scale IV), shall act as the competent authority under the regulations in respect of Officer employees lower in rank and status than such Competent Authority.